Who's That in the White House?

The Modern Years

1969 to 2001

RICHARD M.
NIXON

GERALD R.
FORD

JAMES E.
CARTER

RONALD
REAGAN

GEORGE
BUSH

WILLIAM
CLINTON

by Rose Blue and Corinne J. Naden

RSVP
RAINTREE
STECK-VAUGHN
PUBLISHERS
The Steck-Vaughn Company

Austin, Texas

*To the memory of Mary Lee Graeme and to Rose's mom,
two very gutsy ladies.*

Published by Raintree Steck-Vaughn Publishers, an imprint of Steck-Vaughn Company

Publishing Director: Walter Kossmann   **Project Manager:** Lyda Guz
Editor: Shirley Shalit   **Electronic Production:** Scott Melcer
Consultant: Andrew Frank, University of Florida   **Photo Editor:** Margie Foster

Library of Congress Cataloging-in-Publication Data
Blue, Rose.
The modern years 1969 to 2001 / by Rose Blue and Corinne J. Naden.
p. cm. — (Who's that in the White House?)
Includes bibliographical references and index.
Summary: Describes the lives and political careers of the six men who have served as president during the last three decades of the twentieth century: Richard Nixon, Gerald Ford, Jimmy Carter, Ronald Reagan, George Bush, and Bill Clinton.
ISBN 0-8172-4305-4
1. Presidents — United States — Biography — Juvenile literature. 2. United States — Politics and government — 1945–1989 — Juvenile literature. 3. United States — Politics and government — 1989– — Juvenile literature. [1. Presidents. 2. United States — Politics and government — 1945–1989. 3. United States — Politics and government — 1989–]
I. Naden, Corinne J. II. Title. III. Series: Blue, Rose. Who's that in the White House?
E176.1.B673 1998
973'.09'9 — dc21
97-15039
CIP AC

Acknowledgments
The authors wish to thank Harold C. Vaughan of Fort Lee, New Jersey, for his critical reading of the manuscript.
Photography credits: Cover White House Photo; Title page (top row, bottom left) National Portrait Gallery—The Smithsonian Institution, (bottom right) White House Photo, (bottom center) Bush Presidential Library; p. 5 Reuters/Corbis-Bettmann; p. 7 National Portrait Gallery, The Smithsonian Institution; p. 8 AP/Wide World Photos; p. 9 The Bettmann Archive; p. 10 UPI/Corbis-Bettmann; p. 11 Brown Brothers; pp. 12, 16, 17 UPI/Corbis-Bettmann; p. 20 National Portrait Gallery, The Smithsonian Institution; p. 21 AP/World Wide Photos; p. 22 Culver Pictures; p. 24 UPI/Corbis-Bettmann; p. 26 © Newsweek, Inc. p. 27 National Portrait Gallery, The Smithsonian Institution; pp. 29, 33 UPI/Corbis-Bettmann; p. 34 AP/Wide World Photos; p. 36 UPI/Corbis-Bettmann; p. 38 Reuters/Corbis-Bettmann; p. 40 National Portrait Gallery, The Smithsonian Institution; p. 42 Culver Pictures; pp. 43, 45, 49 UPI/Corbis-Bettmann; p. 50 Agence France Presse/Corbis-Bettmann; p. 52 NASA; p. 54 Reuters/Corbis-Bettmann; p. 56 © Robert Grossman; p. 57 Bush Presidential Library; p. 60 AP/Wide World Photos; pp. 61, 65 UPI/Corbis-Bettmann; pp. 67, 68 (top) Reuters/Corbis-Bettmann; p. 68 (bottom) AP/Wide World Photos; p. 70 © Robert Grossman; p. 71 White House Photos; p. 73 International Media Exchange/Corbis-Bettmann; p. 75 AP/Wide World Photos; p. 77 AFP/Corbis-Bettmann; p. 78 AP/Wide World Photos; p. 84 Reuters/Corbis-Bettmann.
Cartography: GeoSystems, Inc.

Contents:

Prologue
Two Hundred Eight...and Growing 4

One
Nixon: Troubled Man, Troubled Time 7

Two
Ford: A New Way to the White House 20

Three
Meet Jimmy Carter from Plains 27

Four
Reagan on Center Stage 40

Five
Bush: A Long Wait for a Short Term 57

Six
Bill Clinton, Dark Horse from Arkansas 71

**Important Facts and Events in the Terms
of Presidents Thirty-Seven Through Forty-Two** 87

Glossary 90

Further Reading 91

Index 92

Two Hundred Eight...and Growing

*W*hen William Jefferson Clinton took the oath of office on January 20, 1997, he said the same words George Washington said nearly 208 years before. The forty-second President, just like the first, raised his right hand and swore that he would

...faithfully execute the Office of President of
the United States, and will to the best of my
Ability, preserve, protect and defend the
Constitution of the United States.

The same words 208 years apart...from the late eighteenth century to almost the end of the twentieth. From 1789 to 1997, each succeeding President has promised to preserve, protect, and defend. There's a nice feeling of permanence and stability in that. To be sure, 208 years of history isn't so much compared to, say, that of China or Egypt or Greece. Yet, for Americans in the modern era, it is proof that the marvelous experiment in representative democracy is still working...and still growing.

The first President of the United States would surely have been proud to see the latest leader take the same oath of office. He would have been shocked as well. The oath was the same, the title was the same, but just about everything else was different. For starters, Washington would have been surprised at the date. He had been inaugurated on April 30, 1789, and all following Presidents took the oath in March until Franklin Roosevelt in 1933. From then on, Inauguration Day has been January 20. Washington became President in New York City and John Adams in Philadelphia. Since then, all Presidents have been inaugurated in Washington, D.C. Washington certainly would have been surprised at Clinton's inaugural suit! The first President wore brown breeches that ended at the knee and

4

A general overview of the Capitol building in Washington, D.C., during Bill Clinton's first inauguration January 20, 1993. Note that the two outer flags have 13 stars in a circle, the next two have 25 and flank the current flag with 50 stars.

long white silk stockings to the ceremony. Clinton wore long dark trousers and it is doubtful that his socks were white.

After the inauguration in 1997, the President went home to the White House. It wasn't even there when Washington was President and wasn't completed until 1800 when John and Abigail Adams moved in. Actually, it wasn't even completed then, according to the second First Lady. Mrs. Adams complained that the White House was so damp it aggravated her rheumatism. A meticulous housekeeper, she was also highly annoyed because no one had thought to put a washline out in the yard. So, she hung the family's laundry in the huge—and unfinished—East Room. Presumably, she would be more pleased with the use of the East Room today, as it is the site for elegant state dinners.

Washington was the leader of a country with 13 states and fewer than four million people. Clinton governs 50 states and a population of more than 260 million!

Much else might have surprised George Washington about his beloved United States of America. In 208 years, the country has grown not only in size but in complexity, in wealth, in strength, in problems, in turmoil, and in just about anything else. The people who led and continue to lead this nation through the modern era have concerns Washington could not possibly have dreamed of. Should we build a space station on the moon? How can we provide health care for every citizen? Is television a good or bad influence on the population? What effect will high technology, such as the Internet, have on the average American? Is nuclear war still a real possibility?

The modern years have modern problems. The United States was a weak, little-respected nation when Washington took office. Today, it is the world's superpower, respected by some, feared by others. There have been many differences and great changes in the world and in the country from Washington's time until today. But in some ways the men who have led this nation through the modern era wrestle with the same problems. Like Washington, their goals are the preservation, stability, growth, and health of their country. To a greater or lesser degree, according to their greater or lesser abilities, these modern Presidents have changed U.S. direction or altered U.S. history with decisions they made from that stately old building on Pennsylvania Avenue known as the White House.

Chapter One

Nixon: Troubled Man, Troubled Time

Richard Milhous Nixon
(1969-1974)

In the list of Presidents of the United States, from the beginning of its history until today, surely one of the most controversial— and complicated—was number thirty seven: Richard Milhous Nixon. He was a naval officer, a member of both the House and Senate, and a two-term vice president under Dwight Eisenhower. But he was defeated in races for President and for governor of California and vowed never to run again. A strong anticommunist, he earned the title of "Tricky Dick" for his ruthless political tactics, but bounced back to enter the White House. Psychologists and historians spoke of him as "suspicious and secretive," a man "torn by inner conflict," a "compulsive liar." He was applauded for his fine grasp of international affairs, but lost the respect of his country for his involvement in America's greatest political scandal—Watergate. Facing almost certain impeachment, Richard Nixon was the only U.S. President in history to resign from office.

This controversial public figure was born in Yorba Linda, California, on January 9, 1913. He was the second of five sons born to Francis and Hannah Milhous Nixon. Two of his brothers died of tuberculosis, one at age seven, the other at age 23. His father was a quarrelsome man who tried his hand at running gas stations and grocery stores. At one time, he moved the family to a farm in Pennsylvania. Nixon's mother was a devout Quaker and wanted her second son to grow up to be a missionary.

The future President had some impressive relatives on the family tree. His mother's ancestors dated back to King Edward III (1312–1377) of England. Great-great-great grandfather Nixon crossed the Delaware with George Washington, and great-grandfather Nixon died at Gettysburg during the Civil War.

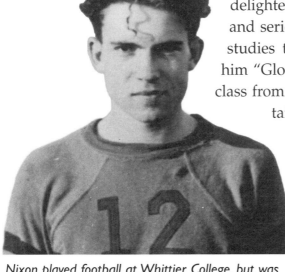

From a roly-poly 11 pounds at birth, Richard grew to be nearly six feet tall, with thick eyebrows, a ski nose, and sagging jowls that delighted cartoonists. As a child, he was quiet and serious. He became so serious about his studies that his California classmates called him "Gloomy Gus." He graduated first in his class from Whittier High in 1930 and was captain of the debating team at Whittier College, where he also played second string on the football team. Graduating number two in his class earned him a scholarship to Duke University Law School, where he graduated third in his class in 1937.

Nixon played football at Whittier College, but was not a letter winner. He was known as "the most spirited bench warmer on the team."

Back in Whittier, Nixon began to practice law and in 1938 met a pretty would-be actress, Thelma "Pat" Ryan. After graduation from the University of Southern California, she had some bit parts in the movies and then went on to teach at Whittier High. When Nixon found out that the new teacher was active in the local theater, he won a part opposite her and proposed the same night. Pat Nixon later said, "I thought he was nuts." Nuts or not, they were married in 1940 and eventually had two daughters.

Nixon left law in 1940 to become president of a local juice manufacturing company. With him at the helm, the company failed in two years. His next job was with the federal government, which discouraged him even more, so he quit and joined the navy. Lieutenant Commander Nixon served in the South Pacific during World War II and was cited for excellent service.

Back home and ready to try politics, Nixon was elected to the House of Representatives from California. An ardent anticommunist, the young congressman quickly jumped into the national spotlight as a member of the House Un-American Activities Committee. This committee was a product of the intense rivalry that developed between the United States and the Soviet Union known as the Cold War.

Although Russians and Americans had been allies during World War II, their alliance began to unravel soon after the fighting stopped. The United States feared the growth of communism in Europe. The Soviets made no secret of their wish to spread the Communist doctrine worldwide. During 1948–1953, the Cold War reached its peak. The Soviet Union exploded its first atomic warhead in 1949, increasing U.S. fears of nuclear war. Also in 1949, the United States and its allies established the North Atlantic Treaty Organization (NATO) to resist Soviet domination in Europe. Distrust and fear between the two countries escalated.

The so-called Red Scare permeated American life. U.S. citizens—prompted by Senator Joseph R. McCarthy of Wisconsin—began looking for Communists around every corner. There could be no greater disgrace in America than to be accused of being a Communist or even of "being soft" on communism. Nixon found "his Communist" in

In 1970, the Nixon family poses for this family portrait in the White House Rose Garden. (Left to right) Tricia, President Nixon, Mamie Eisenhower, Pat Nixon, Julie Nixon and David Eisenhower.

Representative Nixon (Republican-California) looks over microfilm discovered in a hollowed-out pumpkin on the Maryland farm of Whittaker Chambers. This evidence was instrumental in the final conviction of Alger Hiss for spying. Robert Stripling, chief investigator for the House Un-American Activities Committee, is holding the film.

Alger Hiss, a former government official accused of leaking secrets to the Russians. The future President was relentless in his grilling of Hiss, who denied all charges but was convicted of giving false testimony.

Nixon, at age 37, was first called "Tricky Dick" when he ran for the Senate from California. His opponent in 1950 was another House member, Democrat Helen Gahagan Douglas. Nixon flooded the state with some 500,000 pink-colored sheets—Red Scare again—implying that Douglas's record linked her to the Communists. He also referred to her as the Pink Lady. It worked. Nixon won by 680,000 votes. Today, American voters are unfortunately all too used to political smears and so-called dirty tactics. But this was still a fairly new concept in the early postwar era. However, this time, a small California newspaper, the *Independent Review*, called foul play and dubbed the new senator as "tricky."

His campaign may have tagged him with a shady nickname, but Nixon's dogged pursuit of Communists got him the number two spot with war hero Dwight Eisenhower on the presidential election ticket of 1952. The senator would help to emphasize the Republican's anticommunist platform. It also helped that Nixon was from a western state. Even more than today, presidential hopefuls tended to be careful about "balancing" the ticket geographically, matching a northerner with a southerner, or easterner to westerner.

However, this match almost backfired for Eisenhower. The *New York Post* charged Nixon with spending secret money from secret contributors for his personal use. This was illegal. Eisenhower was urged to dump Nixon. Instead, Ike gave him a chance to clear himself. So, Nixon went on television, his family at his side, and delivered his now famous "Checkers" speech. He said there was indeed such a fund but not for his personal use. Then he listed all his modest personal assets and pointed to six-year-old daughter Tricia's cocker spaniel, named Checkers. He admitted the dog was a gift, but emotionally declared that they were going to keep him.

Nixon was the nation's vice president for the next eight years. He presided over the Cabinet while Ike recovered from a heart attack in 1955 and exchanged heated remarks with Russian leader Nikita Khrushchev during a trip to Moscow in 1959. Because the

In July 1959, Vice President Nixon debates Soviet Premier Nikita Khrushchev (center) during a visit to Moscow.

two men were standing in an exhibition of an American house, the argument was known as the Kitchen Debate.

When Eisenhower left the White House after two terms, Nixon was the logical Republican choice for the 1960 election. But the defeat was bitter when he lost to John Kennedy by only 120,000 popular votes. Two years later, Nixon lost another close one, this time the race against California's governor, Democrat Edmund "Pat" Brown. After that, Nixon really showed his disappointment and bitterness as he took on the press, lashing out at them for 16 years of attacks in print. His political career was over, he said, and so was their fun, for they "won't have Nixon to kick around any more."

However, his retirement lasted only until the presidential election of 1968 when, with Maryland's Spiro Agnew as running mate, Richard Milhous Nixon at last reached his goal. He defeated Hubert H. Humphrey of Minnesota to become the thirty-seventh President of the United States.

At once, the new President announced the Nixon Doctrine. He would reduce the number of U.S. troops overseas, substituting economic aid and military equipment to help smaller nations defend themselves. He tried, mostly unsuccessfully, to deal with growing inflation, the country's number one domestic problem. His most significant foreign achievement was reopening communication with Communist China after 21 years. One of the proudest moments of his presidency occurred on July 20, 1969,

After astronauts Neil Armstrong, Michael Collins, and Edwin Aldrin returned to Earth from the moon landing in 1969, President Nixon talks to them in their isolation quarters aboard the USS *Hornet.*

when Nixon spoke to Astronaut Neil Armstrong. Nixon was in the White House and Armstrong was on the moon. The commander of *Apollo 11* had just become the first human being in all history to set foot on the moon. Said Armstrong, "That's one small step for a man, one giant leap for mankind." And so it was...the crowning achievement of the U.S. space program.

The war between North and South Vietnam in Southeast Asia, which had begun in 1955, continued under Nixon. Communist North Vietnam wanted to unite the two countries under its leadership. South Vietnam and the United States were opposed. This became a long and bitter struggle. The United States, fearing the spread of communism in Asia, backed the South Vietnam government of Ngo Dinh Diem and began to supply ever increasing economic and military support. With each new U.S. President, American involvement grew. By 1968, there were nearly 400,000 U.S. military personnel in Vietnam. As the war dragged on, more and more Americans began to protest U.S. involvement.

Once in office, Nixon did reduce the number of U.S. troops in Vietnam, but he expanded the fighting into Cambodia and Laos. In the meantime, America was growing ever more violent in its antiwar protests. The most dramatic and shocking instance occurred in the spring of 1970 at Kent State University in Ohio when state national guardsmen were sent on campus to stop an antiwar demonstration. They ended up killing four students and wounding nine. It seemed as though the country had gone mad over the faraway war that had come home.

The terrible ordeal ended with a Communist victory in Vietnam. The peace treaty was signed in Paris in January 1973. Some 58,000 Americans died in the war nobody wanted, and it cost the United States $110 billion. Vietnam veterans came home to hostility and indifference as citizens took out their anger and frustration on those who had heeded their obligation to fight. The anger and hostility have been a long time leaving as has the bitterness still felt by those who fought. Some of it was alleviated with the dedication, in 1982, of the Vietnam Veterans Memorial in Washington, D.C. On the V-shaped black granite wall are listed the names of all those who died in the war. Since then, two additions have been made to the memorial site. A sculpture called *Three Servicemen* was dedicated in 1984, and ten years later, the nearly 12,000 women who served were honored by the Vietnam Women's Memorial.

It was election time again in 1972. In one of the biggest landslide victories in U.S. history, Nixon defeated Democrat George McGovern, who managed only 17 electoral votes against Nixon's 520.

McGovern didn't really have a chance. For one thing, he was seen by much of the population as too far left—meaning for some too lenient with communism. He offered a broad program of liberal social and economic reforms at home, but the American public was not in a spending or reform frame of mind. In addition, McGovern got caught in his own words. He campaigned as a man who would not compromise for political gain. But when his running mate, Thomas Eagleton, admitted to seeing a psychiatrist—a definite political no-no at that time—McGovern dumped him. That smacked of compromising for political gain, and it was the kiss of political death for McGovern.

The second term of Richard Milhous Nixon should have been his crowning achievement. He had survived "Tricky Dick" and Checkers and being "kicked around" by the press. He was gaining admiration for his dealings with the Soviet Union, which had led to a nuclear arms limitation agreement, and for his more open policy with Red China. His long up-and-down career should have been topped by four productive, respected years. Instead, Nixon's second term is forever linked to the worst scandal ever in U.S. political history. It is known as Watergate.

Actually, the nightmare began before Nixon was even elected for a second term. In the early morning hours of June 17, 1972, five agents of the Committee to Reelect the President (CREEP) were arrested for burglarizing Democratic National Headquarters. The Democrats had set up shop in the Watergate apartment complex in Washington, D.C. The White House dismissed the whole thing as a "third-rate burglary attempt," and most of the country didn't think much of it either—at first.

However, the story just wouldn't go away. Over the next two years, newspaper reporters, notably Bob Woodward and Carl Bernstein of the *Washington Post*, kept turning over rocks and finding political bugs. A Senate Select Committee on Watergate was impaneled to look into the matter, chaired by Democratic Senator Sam Ervin of North Carolina. By now, people were starting to pay attention. Eventually, the investigations produced a number of charges, among them: (1) eavesdropping devices had been secretly installed in the Democratic offices at Watergate by officials of Nixon's presidential campaign, (2) the Republicans had set up a "dirty tricks" squad to cause trouble among Democratic candidates during the 1972 election, (3) some person, or persons, in the White House were trying to cover up criminal acts related to Watergate by paying "hush money," and apparently the President knew about it, and (4) the Nixon White House had an "enemies list." On it were business leaders, news and government people, and show business personalities, such as Carol Channing and Paul Newman.

With each breaking story or new accusation, President Nixon denied any knowledge or any wrongdoing. Yet, his own White House lawyer, John Dean, declared that Nixon may not have actually authorized the Watergate break-in but certainly knew about it. Not so, maintained the President.

Perhaps the truth never would have come out. After all, it was the President's word against Dean's, or the word of White House officials against accusers. But where was the proof?

Who would have thought it would be found on an audio tape? In one of those life-is-stranger-than-fiction events,

In July 1973, H.R. Haldeman, former chief of staff to President Nixon, begins his testimony before the Senate Watergate Committee.

investigators discovered that the President had long been taping conversations at the White House, presumably to write his memoirs. Nixon refused to turn over the tapes to the Senate Committee. He finally had to—most reluctantly—on orders from the Supreme Court. The tapes supported what John Dean had said and branded the President as untruthful. In addition, eighteen and a half minutes of the tapes had been erased. That made Nixon look even more guilty.

One after another, those involved with the White House went down in disgrace—chief of staff H.R. Haldeman, chief domestic affairs adviser John D. Ehrlichman, special counsel Charles Colson, CREEP counsel G. Gordon Liddy, and many more. It was all inching closer and closer to the President.

When things looked as though they couldn't get worse, they did. Now Nixon lost his vice president, Spiro Agnew. A rigid law-and-order man, Agnew branded protesting college students as "impudent snobs" and—to the delight of all media personnel—referred to newspeople as "nattering nabobs of negativism." But in August 1973, he was charged with accepting bribes when he was governor of Maryland. Agnew resigned.

That left the vice president's spot open. So, for the first time, part of the Twenty-Fifth Amendment, ratified in February 1967, came into play. It authorized the President to fill the number two position, if it became empty. After the assassination of John Kennedy in 1963, Vice President Lyndon Johnson stepped into the presidency. Therefore, there was no vice president until 1964, when Johnson was elected with Hubert Humphrey of Minnesota as his running mate. Now, in 1973, with Agnew gone, Nixon picked Gerald R. Ford of Michigan as vice president. Ford was a long-time member of the House and its minority leader when he was chosen.

By July 1974, the Watergate proceedings had advanced so far that the House Judiciary Committee approved impeachment proceedings against Richard Nixon. Impeachment is a criminal charge brought against a public official by a legislative body.

In 1974, Nixon faced three articles of impeachment. (1) He had obstructed justice by withholding evidence and making false statements. (2) He had abused power and interfered with the Watergate investigation. (3) He had failed to obey congressional subpoenas.

There was no way out for the beleaguered President. He was certain to be impeached, the ultimate disgrace. And so, for the first time in U.S. history, a President resigned. Richard Nixon did so on the evening of August 8, effective the following morning. He did not confess, saying only that he had made "errors of judgment." Nearly the entire country stared at history in the making on the television screen as Richard and Pat Nixon left the grounds of the White House in a helicopter. They left behind a newly installed thirty-eighth President

After his resignation as President, Nixon waves with both arms as he boards a helicopter on the White House lawn August 9, 1974, for the first leg of the flight to California and his return to being a private citizen.

of the United States and a new First Lady, Gerald and Betty Ford.

Nixon was never convicted of any wrongdoing in Watergate. He was pardoned by President Ford that September. The former President and his wife retired to San Clemente, California. In 1981, they settled in the small suburban community of Park Ridge, New Jersey, where Pat Nixon died in 1993. Nixon spent several years writing his memoirs as well as books on international affairs. He was forever scarred by Watergate and blamed for much of the mistrust of government that still lingers in the United States. But in the area of foreign policy, he remained respected and even gave advice to the Presidents who followed him. Nixon died on April 22, 1994.

Why Watergate? And why get caught with evidence on tape? Why break into Democratic headquarters at all? Nixon was so far ahead in the 1972 presidential election polls that he stood little chance of losing. An even bigger why is why the tapes? Why didn't the President just destroy them right away?

Probably no one ever really knew the truth except the President himself. Some experts say it was his ego. He couldn't believe that he would be convicted or indicted or impeached. After all, he *was* the President. He just didn't think it would happen. But it did. Here was a government leader whose whole life was politics, who bounced back time and again from defeat to reach the top of the world's biggest political ladder. Here was a man who wanted so much to be President—perhaps at any cost. The cost turned out to be disgrace as the only President in the country's history to resign. It was a troubled time for the nation, and Richard Nixon was a troubled man for the time.

Names in the News in Nixon's Time

Neil Armstrong (1930–):

Ohio-born astronaut, first human to walk on the moon, during historic *Apollo 11* mission, July 20, 1969.

Clare Booth Luce (1903–1987):

New York-born editor, playwright, congresswoman from Connecticut (1942–1946). Served on Nixon's Foreign Intelligence Advisory Board (1973).

George McGovern (1922–):

Representative and senator from South Dakota. Lost presidential election to Nixon (1968) by wide margin. Targeted as too liberal and too radical.

John Mitchell (1913–1988).

Born New York, law partner of Nixon and later his attorney general. Served 19 months in prison for conspiracy and obstruction of justice in Watergate scandal.

George Wallace (1919–):

Governor of Alabama (1963–1967), obtained national recognition by standing in the door of the University of Alabama to prevent black enrollment. Opposed Nixon in 1968 election as head of American Independent party. Paralyzed by gunshot wound in 1972. Reelected governor of Alabama in 1982.

Chapter Two

Ford: A New Way to the White House

Gerald R. Ford (1974-1977)

*I*t's a distinction of sorts and it's in the history books. Gerald R. Ford is the only U.S. President who wasn't elected—that is, he never won an election for President or vice president. Eight men—John Tyler, Millard Fillmore, Andrew Johnson, Chester Arthur, Theodore Roosevelt, Calvin Coolidge, Harry Truman, and Lyndon Johnson—all took over the unexpired term of an elected President. But all of those men had been elected to the vice president's job. Ford was not an elected vice president when he became President. Richard Nixon had selected him, under the Twenty-Fifth Amendment, when the elected vice president, Spiro Agnew, had to resign in 1973. The following August, Nixon resigned and Ford became the thirty-eighth President of the United States without collecting one single vote.

Ford has not only had a few job changes in his lifetime, but some name changes, too. He was born Leslie Lynch King, Jr., in Omaha, Nebraska, on July 14, 1913. After a divorce, his mother took her infant son to Grand Rapids, Michigan, where she married Gerald Rudolf Ford, who adopted the boy. Later, Ford changed the spelling of his middle name to Rudolph.

Jerry had a typical midwestern middle-class childhood. His most traumatic event occurred at age 17 when he met his biological father. Leslie King walked into a Grand Rapids restaurant where Ford was working and after an awkward lunch, gave the young man $25 and left in his luxury car. A well-to-do wool

20

merchant, King did not see his son again until Ford was in college. The son bitterly resented his biological father's indifference. In contrast, he regarded his stepfather, a paint store owner, as a man of great integrity and the strongest influence on his life.

A friendly, open, and honest youngster, Jerry Ford grew to be six feet tall and athletic. He made the honor society at South High in East Grand Rapids and was the football team's star center. His grades earned him a partial scholarship at the University of Michigan. He waited on tables for extra money and, as a senior, was named the most valuable player on the Wolverines football team. After playing center in the 1935 College All-Stars game against the Chicago Bears, he was

Ford played football for the University of Michigan in 1934. He won three varsity letters as a lineman and was voted most valuable player. He later took part in the Shrine Bowl and Pro-All Stars post-season games.

offered pro football contracts by both the Detroit Lions and the Green Bay Packers. Ford turned them down for law school, which was probably just as well since he developed weak knees from too many gridiron injuries.

From Michigan, Ford went to Yale where he was hired as an assistant football coach. What with coaching and other jobs—he spent some time as a male model—he did not get his law degree until 1941. Shortly after, he was admitted to the Michigan bar, meaning he passed the exam to practice law in that state.

Two years later, Ford was in the South Pacific during World War II as a naval gunnery officer aboard the USS *Monterey*, a light aircraft carrier. Nearly tossed overboard during a typhoon, Ford earned ten battle stars aboard the carrier at such places as Okinawa and Wake Island. He left the service in 1946 as a lieutenant commander.

President Ford and his family pose in the White House. Standing behind the President and Elizabeth "Betty" Ford are Susan, Steven, John, and Michael, and Michael's wife, Gayle.

In 1947, Ford, now age 34, began to date a newly divorced former dancer and model, Elizabeth Anne Bloomer, age 29. They were married the next year, right in the middle of Ford's first run for Congress. In fact, he had attended a political rally just before getting to the church and met his wife-to-be at the altar with muddy shoes. Their two-day honeymoon was somewhat unusual, too. They went to a Michigan-Northwestern football game one afternoon and a rally for presidential hopeful Thomas Dewey that evening.

The Fords eventually had four children. Michael is a minister; John, a journalist; Steven, an actor; and daughter Susan, a photographer. She was in school when her father entered the White House and she served as hostess while her mother was recovering from a cancer operation.

As First Lady, Betty Ford spoke out for abortion rights and aid to the mentally retarded. She earned praise for her candor in openly discussing her bout with breast cancer and her struggles with alcohol and painkilling drugs. After seeking treatment for her own alcohol addiction, she opened the Betty Ford Clinic, now a well-known recovery center.

Gerald Ford was elected to the House of Representatives on his first try in 1949 and was reelected 12 times. By 1973, he was the House minority leader, meaning the head of the party not in power—at that time, the Republicans. Ford was well respected in Congress, regarded as a moderate conservative on most matters. He was on the Warren Commission that investigated the assassination of President Kennedy. He attacked President

Johnson's conduct of the war in Vietnam and was a general backer of President Nixon's policies.

Ford was plucked out of the House by Nixon after the resignation of Spiro Agnew as vice president. Reportedly, Nixon had first considered choosing former Governor John Connally of Texas or Governor Nelson Rockefeller of New York or Governor Ronald Reagan of California, but for various reasons rejected them. Instead, he settled on moderate Jerry Ford to fill the office of vice president. Ford had a spotless record and was well liked in Congress.

Indeed, the Congress overwhelmingly approved Nixon's choice. Ford took the oath of office on December 6, 1973. Nixon assured his new vice president that the tapes, which the President was refusing to give up at the time, would clear him of any suspicion. He asked if Ford would like to listen to them. Ford declined.

Less than a year later, at 12:03 P.M. on August 9, 1974, Gerald Ford was sworn in as the thirty-eighth President by Chief Justice Warren Burger in the East Room of the White House. Said Ford, commenting on Watergate, "Our long national nightmare is over."

Not quite, of course. It would be a long time before the scandal of Watergate and the distrust of government began to subside. Ford did not help the cause very much by granting former President Nixon a full pardon "for all offenses against the United States" on September 8, 1974. That is one of the reasons cited as causing Ford's defeat in the 1976 election. But the President maintained that the humiliation of Nixon's resignation was punishment enough. He also used the Twenty-Fifth Amendment to appoint his own—and unelected—vice president, Nelson Rockefeller of New York.

The war in Vietnam was finally winding down in early 1975 when Ford ordered the airlift of thousands of anticommunist refugees, mostly to America. In May, Cambodian gunboats took control of the U.S. merchant ship *Mayaguez*. Ford called it an "act of piracy" and sent in the marines to recover the ship. They did.

An American helicopter evacuates Americans and foreign nationals from the top of a building in Saigon just prior to the city's takeover by Vietcong troops in April 1975. Most were airlifted to U.S. Navy ships off the Vietnamese coast.

At home, Ford was generally—although slowly—successful at curbing the inflation that had grown steadily during the Nixon administration. He tried to heal the rift caused by the war in Vietnam by granting clemency to the thousands who had sought to evade the draft. They were required to swear an oath of allegiance and perform two years of public service, but many thought that was admitting to wrongdoing and refused.

Friendly, nice guy Jerry Ford was often ribbed by the press for his seeming clumsiness, despite his athletic prowess. If the President tripped up a step or over a blade of grass, photographers were there to record the incident. Ford took it all with rather good grace and also survived two assassination attempts with relative calm. Both attempts were made by women and both of them occurred in September 1975. Lynette "Squeaky" Fromme fired a Colt .45 at the President in Sacramento just as he was about to shake her hand. He was lucky. Although there was an ammunition clip in the gun, there was no bullet in the chamber. A follower of California mass murderer Charles Manson, Fromme was the first to be convicted on the 1965 law that decreed life imprisonment for attempting to take the life of a President. She is still in jail. The second attempt was in San Francisco. Sara Jane Moore, a political activist, missed the President by a few feet. She also is still in jail.

Would-be assassins aside, people generally seemed to like Jerry Ford. Senator Robert Dole of Kansas said Ford put the nation's economy back on the road to good health. Henry Kissinger, whom Ford kept on as secretary of state when Nixon resigned, called him an American of "unquestioned integrity." Kissinger's praise was not taken lightly. He is recognized as a major influence in shaping American foreign policy from 1969 to 1976 and is highly respected as an expert in international and national security affairs. Despite a good deal of negative press, many historians look upon Gerald Ford as a sort of welcome buffer after the nastiness, distrust, and backbiting of Watergate. His amiable honesty and good nature poured some soothing oil on the troubled land. For a time anyway.

Then it was 1976, and Ford decided to run for President in his own right. He barely won his party's nomination from conserv-ative Ronald Reagan and faced Jimmy Carter in the presidential race. Ford lost a fairly close one, 297 to 240 electoral votes and a popular vote difference of less than two million.

A disappointed Ford retired to California to write his memoirs and make speaking appearances. Although he briefly considered a return to public life as Ronald Reagan's running mate in 1980, he has stayed out of the political arena where he made history for such a short time. In 1981, however, Ford was briefly back in the limelight as part of an historic group that attended the funeral of Egypt's assassinated leader, Anwar Sadat. For the first time in his-tory, four residents of the White House were photographed together: Ronald Reagan, then in office, and former Presidents Richard Nixon, Jimmy Carter, and Gerald Ford.

In a speech to the public after becoming President, Ford summed up his best feelings about government. In so doing, he also summed up Gerald R. Ford in a way that might have made George Washington proud. Said Ford, "I expect to follow my instincts of openness and candor with full confidence that hon-esty is always the best policy in the end."

Names in the News in Ford's Time

Henry Kissinger (1933–):

Secretary of state under Nixon, held same post under Ford. Noted for "shuttle diplomacy"—constant, back-and-forth travel to touchy international spots to ease tensions, especially in the Middle East during the Arab-Israeli war of 1973. He helped to bring about the Sinai accord, a period of peace between Egypt and Israel.

In 1973, cartoonist Ranan Lurie showed a duplicitous Secretary of State Henry Kissinger apparently revealing hands to both Israel's Golda Meir and Egypt's Anwar Sadat.

Nelson A. Rockefeller (1908–1979):

New York-born son of industrialist John D. Rockefeller. Chosen as vice president by Ford under provisions of the Twenty-Fifth Amendment after Nixon resigned and Ford became President.

Eudora Welty (1909–):

One of the South's most noted writers, born in Mississippi. Her *The Optimist's Daughter* won the Pulitzer Prize—many said long overdue—in 1973.

Chapter Three

Meet Jimmy Carter from Plains

James Earl Carter (1977-1981)

*H*e calls himself Jimmy and signs his name Jimmy Carter. Unofficially, he must be the most outwardly relaxed man who ever sat in the Oval Office. In modern memory, he was surely the most informal. He generally presided over Cabinet meetings in a cardigan sweater and more than once was caught carrying his own luggage onto the presidential plane, *Air Force One*. But as political enemies often learned, don't let that soft down-home Georgia drawl fool you. Softies don't get to the White House, and James Earl Carter, Jr., is no softie.

He is, rather, a complex personality. A man of moderate height and build, he appears shy, his toothy grin easy and broad. He speaks softly and likes to wear a red tie—when he has to wear a tie at all. But underneath the shyness and compassion for others dwells a supremely confident man of steel. He is extremely self-disciplined and rarely loses his temper in front of others. But if he's displeased, he can cut you down with a bit of sarcasm.

Above all, Jimmy Carter is a man who is not afraid to work for what he wants. And that's how he traveled from a peanut farm in Plains, Georgia, to a large white house at 1600 Pennsylvania Avenue, in Washington, D.C.

If a good work ethic brings success, young James Earl Carter was on the way at age five. That's when he began selling peanuts on the streets of the small Georgia town where he was born on

October 1, 1924. Carter was the first U.S. President to be born in a hospital. The Carters were rather well-to-do by rural Georgia standards of the time, although their house had neither running water nor electricity. His father, James Earl, Sr., was a peanut farmer and later a state legislator, who believed, as many did at the time, that the races should not mix. His wife was far more liberal. Lillian Gordy Carter, a registered nurse and later a Peace Corps volunteer, tended blacks as well as whites and drew criticism from her neighbors because of it. Generally known as Miss Lilly, she lived to see her oldest child, James Earl, Jr., become President.

Lillian Carter taught her four children the value of education and compassion for others. Jimmy's sister Gloria married and remained in Plains. Ruth became a Baptist evangelist, one who spreads the word of God through sermons and special services. Through her, Carter later became a born-again Christian, a term that designates someone who dedicates him- or herself to following the Christian faith. Billy was something of a character when his older brother was in the White House—a rather free spirit who ran a gas station in Plains and later marketed his own brand of beer.

Jimmy was a well-behaved child. However, his father did spank him once for aiming his BB gun at his sister. He was also a good student who loved to read. Years later in his inaugural address, he pointed out his English teacher, Julia Coleman, as the greatest influence on his education. He did admit, however, that when she first gave him *War and Peace*, the classic Russian novel by Tolstoy, he was quite disappointed to find that it wasn't about cowboys and Indians.

After graduating from Plains High School, where he played on the basketball team, Carter went to Georgia Southwestern College and applied to the U.S. Naval Academy at Annapolis, Maryland. He was accepted in 1943 after taking some catch-up courses in math. Enduring much teasing because of his southern accent, Carter graduated number 59 out of 820 midshipmen in his class of 1946. World War II speeded up academy education.

Lt. Jimmy Carter looks on as Mrs. Willis Manning Thomas, widow of the commander of the submarine Pompano in World War II, prepares to launch a new Navy sub in March 1951. Carter was assigned as an officer aboard the vessel.

Ensign Carter went to war fully intending to spend his life in the navy. He set his sights on becoming chief of naval operations. After two years at sea, he attended submarine school in New London, Connecticut, and joined the nuclear submarine program in 1951. Carter became engineering officer aboard the *Sea Wolf,* one of the first U.S. atomic subs. But in 1953, James Earl, Sr., died and so did Jimmy's naval career. He felt obliged to leave the service and return home to manage the operation of the peanut farm.

This decision did not make Eleanor Rosalynn Smith Carter happy. She and Jimmy had married in 1946 soon after Jimmy graduated from Annapolis. Rosalynn was a Plains native herself who had known her future husband casually all her life. She liked the excitement of navy life and was not anxious to return to small-town Plains. But she did, and her bookkeeping ability helped turn the Carter peanut venture into a prosperous business. Later, in the White House, Rosalynn Carter's advice was highly valued by her husband. She overcame her basic shyness, much in the manner of Eleanor Roosevelt, to speak out on such issues as improvement in mental health programs.

Jimmy and Rosalynn Carter had four children. Jack is a lawyer; James III, called Chip, is a businessman; Jeff is a computer consultant; and Amy was only nine when she went to live in the White House. The public first got a glimpse of her when it was announced that the Carters had decided to send their daughter to a public rather than a private school in the nation's capital. A shy child, she kept a low profile during the Carter presidency and even at Brown University in Rhode Island. So, the public was indeed surprised to hear, some years later, that Amy Carter had been arrested! She and several other Brown students were cited for picketing IBM to protest the company's business dealings with the Republic of South Africa, which at the time had a strict policy of separation of the races. Amy, who was married in 1996, continues to be politically active.

Back in Plains, hard work paid off, and in later years the peanut business made Carter a millionaire. He became active in local affairs and called for racial calm after the Supreme Court's decision in 1954 to desegregate the schools. In 1962, he ran for the state Senate and lost. But Carter cried foul, claiming voter fraud. He proved it, and the election was overturned.

By 1966, Carter had his eyes on the governor's seat. He lost that time, too, but 1970 proved luckier. Carter was a moderate, but so was his opponent, former governor Carl Sanders. So Carter turned more conservative, even inviting the Alabama governor and staunch segregationist, George Wallace, to campaign for him. This more conservative position, however, was short-lived. Also during the campaign, his casual dress came into play. Carter kept referring to his well-dressed opponent as "Cufflinks Carl."

Carter won the election and, despite claims during his conservative campaign, was a moderate governor. "The time for racial discrimination," he said in his inaugural address, "is over." Soon he was being called a leader of the New South. That term has been used over the past century to mean different things, but in Carter's time it indicated a place of racial integration, urban development, liberal politics, and ethnic harmony. This was in great contrast to the poor, segregated, and rural South of slavery and plantation life. Carter himself, southern drawl and all, had come from that poor rural South, but his politics and actions came to symbolize the South of the late twentieth century. In fact, he fostered integration by employing more African Americans in state government and equalizing state funding for rich and poor school districts. This was indeed a change.

Despite his popularity and his New South image, Jimmy Carter remained a little known figure outside of Georgia. In 1974, just two years before he ran for President, he appeared on a then popular television show called "What's My Line." Three contestants, all claiming to be the same person—in this case, Jimmy Carter, governor of Georgia—appeared before a panel of well-known TV personalities. The panel asked questions and tried to guess which one was the actual person. When Carter appeared, his face was so little known that he very nearly stumped the experts.

How do you get from "nobody knows my face" to President in just two years? In Carter's case, you put on a tie and start talking. In late 1974, just before his term as governor was up, Carter declared himself in the presidential race. Talk about a dark horse! That's the term for a candidate who is very little known. Carter was such a dark horse that his name didn't even show up on a possible list of dark horses! But the soft-spoken, shy-appearing man with the southern drawl and polite manners just kept on telling anyone who would listen that what the country needed was to put trust back in government after Vietnam and Watergate.

The political experts paid no attention and went on writing about Morris Udall of Arizona or Henry Jackson of Washington or George Wallace of Alabama—the names that counted, they thought. Then along came the 1976 Iowa and New Hampshire preelection votes. Carter won! The experts were speechless. Who was Carter? Where'd he come from?

By the time the experts had collected their wits, Democrats all over the country were jumping on the Carter bandwagon. He very nearly derailed himself, however, a few months before the Democratic convention. In one speech he said that neighborhoods did have the right to "maintain their ethnic purity" if they could do so without discrimination. This sounded a lot like racism—to some African Americans especially. But the image was softened by the public support of such eminent African Americans as Coretta Scott King, wife of the slain civil rights leader Martin Luther King, Jr., who backed his presidency.

At the convention in July, James Earl Carter won the nomination on the first ballot, and Senator Walter Mondale of Minnesota became his running mate. They faced incumbent President Gerald Ford and Senator Robert Dole of Kansas on the Republican ticket.

Luck always counts in presidential elections, and Carter and the Democrats had a little luck that year. They began the campaign with Ford a good 30 points behind in the polls. Political pollsters take surveys during election campaigns and, according to the results, decide how many points behind or ahead a candidate may be. The Republicans were fighting the lingering image of Watergate and Ford's pardon of Nixon. For the first time in a presidential election, an incumbent President challenged an opposing candidate to a debate. In the second of three debates, Ford made a grave error by stating that "Eastern Europe was free of Soviet domination." At the time, it was anything but. Carter retorted on national TV, "I'd like to see Mr. Ford convince Polish-Americans that they're not under Russian domination." Ford's running mate didn't help much either in his own television debate where Dole blamed Democrats for every war that had occurred throughout the twentieth century.

Jimmy and Rosalynn Carter, with Amy between them, walked down Pennsylvania Ave. from the Capitol to the White House after his inaugural speech in January 1977.

Even so, the Republicans managed to narrow the gap so much by election day that the race was too close to call. But it went to Carter, who became the thirty-ninth President of the United States on January 20, 1977. After his inaugural address, in which he pledged to create a new national spirit of unity and trust, he waved aside the usual presidential limousine. Hand in hand with the new First Lady, he casually walked down Pennsylvania Avenue, waving and smiling at the crowds, on the way to their new home in the White House. The next day, his first official one on the job, he pardoned all those who had evaded the draft during the Vietnam War.

On the homefront, Carter had some success in getting Congress to pass a bill that would help to conserve the nation's energy resources. In general, however, his relationship with those "on the Hill," a term often used to designate both houses of Congress, was rocky. He did stop the dumping of raw sewage into the ocean and set aside more than 100 million acres of Alaskan land for national parks and wilderness areas. In March 1979, a scary breakdown occurred in the cooling system at the Three Mile Island nuclear power plant in Pennsylvania. Suddenly, the future of nuclear power didn't seem quite so bright—nor safe. Carter appointed a commission to investigate the accident and recommend safer controls.

Despite these improvements, the public began to grumble about the President's inability to control high unemployment and a steadily climbing inflation rate. His foreign policy proved more successful, however. Strangely enough, it was Carter's

handling of foreign affairs that brought him his greatest successes and also shortened his years in the White House.

In 1977, with the aid of Carter's patient diplomatic skills,
the United States and Panama signed a treaty after 13 years
of negotiations. It provided for the return of the canal to
Panama by the end of 1999 and guaranteed that the waterway
be neutral thereafter. However, this agreement created a good
deal of controversy. The Democrats hailed the treaty, and the
Republicans were largely outraged at giving up U.S. control.
It became a divisive issue.

That same year there was more general agreement when
the Carter administration established diplomatic relations with
China and agreed to a proposed second arms limitation treaty
with the Soviet Union. However, when the Soviets invaded
Afghanistan that December, the treaty went down to defeat in
the Senate and was never signed.

After the invasion of Afghanistan, Americans for the first
time saw an angry President Carter. In retaliation for the Soviet
invasion, he suspended grain and high tech shipments to the
Soviet Union. He also joined 63 other nations in boycotting the
Olympic Games held in Moscow. Many U.S. athletes were
understandably upset about missing the competition. Yet, most
of the country saw Carter's decision as a sign of American ethi-
cal behavior. The Soviets stayed in Afghanistan until 1989 when
they withdrew in defeat.

Undoubtedly, Carter's most effective accomplishment as
President was his role as peacemaker in the Camp David
Accords of 1978. Since its founding in 1948, Israel had been in a
state of war with Egypt. For some time, Israeli prime minister
Menachem Begin and Egyptian president Anwar Sadat had
been talking peace, but negotiations had come to a halt in
late 1978. At the urging of President Carter, the two men met
at Camp David, the presidential retreat in Maryland, named
for Dwight Eisenhower's grandson. Sadat, especially, liked

Egyptian President Anwar Sadat, Jimmy Carter, and Israeli Prime Minister Menachem Begin clasp hands on the White House lawn after signing the peace treaty between Egypt and Israel, March 26, 1979. Sadat and Begin later were awarded the Nobel Peace Prize.

Carter. He said, "It is because he is so honest with others, that is why I have no difficulty in dealing with him....He is a man...of lofty values—a farmer, like me."

After 13 days in the secluded woods of Camp David, under Carter's intense and patient personal diplomacy, a framework for peace was created. The feat was honored with great television fanfare. Despite some snags, a treaty was signed in March 1979, ending a 31-year state of war between the two nations.

Jimmy Carter came out of the Camp David Accords as a genuine peacemaker, a calm, dignified, rational statesman. It was undoubtedly his finest hour. He wouldn't have many more in the Oval Office.

Things already started to turn sour shortly after the Israel-Egypt accord. In early November 1979, a mob of militant Iranians stormed the U.S. Embassy in the capital city of Teheran and took 60 Americans as hostages. They demanded that the deposed shah of Iran, who was in New York City at the time for medical treatment, be returned to stand trial. Iran's leader, Ayatollah Khomeini, sided with the militants. He released one hostage who was ill and most of the U.S. women, but he refused to turn over the remaining 52 Americans.

So began a global war of nerves. Carter tried diplomacy once again, but it didn't work this time. Despite massive diplomatic

Three American hostages meet the press inside the besieged American Embassy compound in Teheran on November 18, 1979, and optimistically announce that they might be freed in a few days.

and economic pressure, Iran would not budge. The American public grew more and more restless and frustrated as weeks turned into months. The sight of Americans in captivity angered the public and made the President appear helpless. Finally, in late April 1980, Carter sent a military force to free the hostages. This only made things worse. Although the rescuers did land in Iran, the crash of three U.S. helicopters aborted the mission. When the U.S. military tried to leave, two airplanes collided and eight servicemen died. The American armed forces looked like bumblers, which, of course, made the President look even worse. The hostages would remain in captivity in Iran for a total of 444 days and when they were freed, a new leader sat in the White House.

Jimmy Carter did win his party's nomination for the election of 1980. However, even though he was a sitting President—meaning he already held the office—his chances were slim. American voters had soured on his domestic policies, blaming him, among other things, for soaring gasoline prices. But they were especially frustrated with his inability to bring home the hostages. Each day that the U.S. captives stayed in prison, each day that jeering, taunting Iranians were shown on the television screen brought another great blow to American pride.

In his last State of the Union message in January 1980, the President announced a policy of what became known as the Carter Doctrine. It was a warning to the Soviet Union not to try to take a port in the Persian Gulf region just because there was trouble with Iran and Afghanistan. Said Carter, any such attempt would be repelled by any means necessary "including military force."

On Election Day, Carter and Walter Mondale faced the Republican conservative, Ronald Reagan, and his running mate, George Bush. It was no contest. Reagan got 489 electoral votes, Carter, 49. The popular vote count was nearly 44 million to 35 million. The man from Plains was sent home after one term.

Back in Georgia, Carter learned that his family's peanut business had fallen on hard times in his absence. During his years in Washington, his money had been put in a blind trust, which meant that he had no knowledge of or control over his financial dealings while in the White House. This is a common practice in the twentieth century to insure that sitting Presidents do not profit unfairly from their position of leadership.

In retirement, Carter published his memoirs, called *Keeping Faith*, as well as a book entitled *The Blood of Abraham: Insights Into the Middle East*. But his proudest achievement was the establishment of the Carter Presidential Center in Atlanta, Georgia. Besides his presidential library and museum, the center boasts an international aid organization that helps to eradicate disease and increase farming yields throughout the world.

Since the late 1980s, Jimmy Carter has emerged as kind of unofficial elder statesman of U.S. diplomacy and peacemaking. He has been to Nicaragua to aid in the return of Miskito Indians to their homeland. He went to Panama and then to Haiti along with General Colin Powell, at President Clinton's request, to oversee voting procedures, and to Ethiopia to try to bring about a settlement of warring factions. He has also turned painter, carpenter, tiler, and bricklayer. He and former First Lady Rosalynn are part of the Habitat for Humanity, an organization that gives hands-on help to rebuild slum areas and provide people with low-cost rehabilitated housing.

The administration of James Earl Carter, Jr., was not the success that this gentle, intelligent, hardworking, and determined

Former President Jimmy Carter works as a volunteer for the Habitat for Humanity project in southeast Washington, D.C., in June 1992, constructing ten row houses for homeless people.

man of peace seemed to promise. The American people genuinely liked him for his honest efforts to bring out the good in everyone. Yet, they did not have enough confidence in his executive ability to give him a second try. If that causes pain for the man from Plains, it stays well hidden behind the easy grin and the soft Georgia drawl.

Ironically, however, Jimmy Carter's finest moments may well have begun when he left the White House. Carter has used his position as an ex-President to better the world. His religious and humanistic values, which seemed to hinder his effectiveness as a national leader, have brought him great respect and admiration as a man who genuinely works for the betterment of others. James Earl Carter, Jr., who has been called one of the *least* effective of all U.S. Presidents, may well have become the *most* effective of all U.S. ex-Presidents.

Names in the News in Carter's Time

Patricia R. Harris (1924–1985):

First U.S. African American woman ambassador, to Luxembourg, in Johnson administration. Secretary of the Department of Housing and Urban Development (1977–1979) under Carter and first black Cabinet member (1979–1981) as secretary of the Department of Health and Human Services.

Shirley M. Hufstedler (1925–):

California-born first secretary of the Department of Education (1979–1981).

Walter F. Mondale (1928–):

Minnesota-born vice president under Carter, unsuccessful in bid for presidency in 1984. Filled Hubert Humphrey's vacant Senate seat in 1964; compiled liberal voting record.

Chapter Four

Reagan on Center Stage

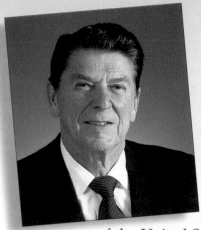

Ronald Wilson Reagan (1981-1989)

*L*awyers have lived in the White House, of course...and teachers...and quite a few military men. Andrew Johnson was a tailor and Herbert Hoover a civil engineer. Jimmy Carter cultivated peanuts. Harry Truman once managed a men's clothing store. But an actor as President of the United States?

Ronald Wilson Reagan was the first resident of the White House to come out of Hollywood! In some 50 films during his 20-year career, he played a good many sentimental romantic roles. Probably his most famous part was the fatally ill football player George Gip who implores his Notre Dame teammates—in an immortal Hollywood line—to "win just one for the Gipper." Although in general, Reagan's acting career was not distinguished, he did draw critical praise for two sensitive performances. Regarded as his best work is the part of Drake McHugh in *Kings Row*, a slice of life in the pre-World War I Midwest (1942). After surgery, McHugh awakens to find his legs have been amputated. His plaintive question "Where's the rest of me?" was later the title of Reagan's 1965 autobiography. On the movie screen, handsome Ronald Reagan was, among other characters, a cowboy, a pilot, a radio announcer, an insurance salesman, a district attorney, and a professor who has a chimp for a child. The latter film, *Bedtime for Bonzo*, through the years brought Reagan the most teasing, which he took in his good-natured way. But never had the former actor played so grand or so important a part as when he was cast as the fortieth President of the United States and eight-year occupant of the White House, with the Oval Office as his backdrop and the whole world as his stage.

As an actor, he never had a stage name. He was born Ronald Wilson Reagan on February 6, 1911, in the family's apartment in Tampico, Illinois. His father, John, was a shoe salesman and liberal Democrat who hated bigotry of any kind. When he first saw his second child, who weighed 10 pounds at birth, he said, "For such a little bit of a fat Dutchman, he makes a heck of a lot of noise, doesn't he?" Ronald Reagan was thereafter called Dutch by family and close friends. His mother, Nelle Wilson Reagan, worked at many jobs to supplement the family income. She made sure that Ronald and his older brother, John, did not resent their father because he was an alcoholic. She got her second child interested in the theater when she organized some local drama recitals. The Reagans moved several times before settling in Dixon, Illinois, when Ronald was nine years old.

Reagan grew into a handsome young man, over six feet tall, with dark wavy hair, blue eyes, and a warm, easy smile. He was a good student at Dixon High School and loved sports, especially football. Later on he admitted that he loved football too much, since his academic average dropped at Eureka College in Illinois where he was admitted on a partial football scholarship. "I let football and other extracurricular activities eat into my study time," he said. He played right guard for the Eureka Golden Tornadoes and also made the track and swim teams.

After graduation in 1932, Reagan decided to become a radio broadcaster. But no one wanted him in the big city of Chicago. He did find a job as weekend sports broadcaster in Davenport, Iowa. Before long, he had made quite a name for himself in the Midwest, becoming the radio voice of Big Ten football and major league baseball. There was no television at the time. With only a telegraph receiver giving him the barest details of a baseball inning,

Reagan's lively imagination and pleasing demeanor fleshed out the game in colorful detail, making up action as he went along. His soft but clear and easy voice would earn him the title of the "Great Communicator" when he became President.

In 1937, a friend of Reagan's arranged for him to take a movie screen test. Warner Brothers, a motion-picture company, signed him at a starting salary of $200 a week. It was the beginning of a 20-year career, which was interrupted when World War II put him on active duty in 1942. He rose to army captain but was barred from combat because of poor eyesight. He was severely nearsighted since childhood. Reagan narrated training films, and the army also allowed him time to star in the 1943 Warner Brothers musical, *This Is the Army*, by Irving Berlin. Movies such as these were regarded as important during World War II in keeping up the spirits and patriotism of those in the military and on the home front.

In his early 20s Ronald Reagan earned his livelihood as a sports announcer for two radio stations in Iowa—WOC in Davenport and WHO in Des Moines.

Before his army service, on January 26, 1940, Reagan had married actress Jane Wyman, whose real name was Sarah Jane Fulks. They had met when they both appeared in the movie *Brother Rat* (1938). It was the idyllic Hollywood marriage of two beautiful people until it ended in divorce in 1948. Ronald Reagan would thus become the first U.S. President to be divorced. Their two children, Maureen, who was later active in politics, and adopted son, Michael, were raised by their mother.

Reagan was heartbroken over the breakup, although he never spoke of the reasons for it. Wyman blamed it on his increasing involvement in politics. Until this point, Reagan had been a Democrat with rather liberal views. Now began his amazing transformation into a staunch and dedicated conservative

Republican. In 1947, he was elected president of the Screen Actors Guild, which is the union for people who work in the film industry. Supposedly, he became an FBI informant, passing on names of those he believed to be pro-Soviet. However, he also criticized Congress for its tactics in tracking down suspected members of the Communist party. The Red Scare was in full force during these postwar years.

In 1952, Reagan, now 41, married his second wife, 30-year-old Nancy Davis, an actress who had been born Anne Frances Robbins in New York City. They were wed in California with actor William Holden as best man. The Reagans appeared in one movie together, *Hell Cats of the Navy* (1957). They would have two children. Patti is a sometime actress, using the name Patti Davis. Ronald, a former ballet dancer, is a television journalist and reporter.

Ronald Reagan and his bride, Nancy Davis, cut their wedding cake with William Holden and his wife, Brenda Marshall, looking on.

By the mid-1950s, Reagan's screen career was fading. Then he became the host of, and actor on, the popular television series, "General Electric Theatre." By the time he left the show in 1962, his political transformation was complete. His views on government and social issues had become more and more conservative over the years, so that he formally changed his political party to Republican. In 1964, he delivered a much praised television speech for the Republican presidential candidate, "Mr. Conservative" himself, Barry Goldwater of Arizona. Goldwater lost the election to Lyndon Johnson. Even Reagan's golden voice could not stem public fears that Goldwater, an extreme anticommunist, would lead the country into war with the Soviet Union.

However, Reagan's speech, although in a losing cause, was not lost on Republican leaders. Unlikely as it seemed to some, the former Hollywood star was now being talked about in serious political circles. For one thing, he had that magic word television gave to politics in the late twentieth century— *charisma!* He was handsome, friendly, likeable, and self-assured without being arrogant. In addition, after years of projecting his voice on film, he was a speechmaker's dream!

And before you could say "two years," he was also governor of California! In 1966, he won over incumbent governor Pat Brown and was reelected in 1970. How did he get from TV host to governor in such a short time? Besides his own personal charisma, Reagan was in the right place at the right time. Californians were grumbling, principally about the state budget and welfare costs. The Brown administration was operating in a deep financial hole. Characterizing the Democrats as "big spenders," Reagan promised to reduce the size and cost of state government. And he did. He also promised a welfare reform package. Once in office, his reforms dropped thousands from the welfare roles and brought in new and tougher requirements to get on welfare in the first place. Surprisingly, he also signed a liberal abortion law and set up state antipollution agencies.

Although he was only modestly successful in getting his programs through the state legislature, Reagan already had his eye on the White House when he left the governor's office in 1975. He announced that he would try to take the 1976 nomination from Gerald Ford, who became President after Nixon's resignation. And Reagan nearly did, falling just 60 votes short at the Republican National Convention in Kansas City, Missouri.

But 1980 was a whole other ball game! Reagan was the dominant figure in Republican politics as the party gathered for its convention in Detroit. He won easily on the first ballot and named George Bush as his running mate.

President Jimmy Carter was running for reelection, but the Democrats knew they were in trouble. The public was displeased with Carter's domestic leadership and dismayed with his inability to bring home the American hostages held in Iran since the preceding November. And as usual, the public was also in the mood for tax cuts and a balanced budget. Reagan promised that he could bring about both, and his ideas

A serious Jimmy Carter listens to Ronald Reagan's response to a question during their televised debate in Cleveland, Ohio, October 28, 1980.

seemed magical. But perhaps most of all, his genial, easily delivered speeches seemed to promise an almost nostalgic return to "good old American values—to mom and apple pie and the traditional American family." The speech also implied that the United States would once again prove itself a world superpower that could battle the "evil empire," as Reagan called the U.S.S.R.

It sounded so good. Americans were weary of the hate and bitterness over Vietnam and shamed by the inability of their leaders to free the hostages in Iran. Where were the good old days? Enough Americans thought they were in the reassuring voice of Ronald Reagan. So, they put him in office with a landslide victory, 489 electoral votes to Carter's 49.

Reagan's first day as the fortieth President of the United States began on a decided upbeat note. The previous November, the militants holding the U.S. hostages had given them over to the Iranian government. The government of Algeria then stepped in as mediator between Iran and the United States. Iran's leader, Khomeini, agreed to give up the hostages if the U.S. government freed Iranian assets being held in the United States. The deal was made. On Inauguration Day, January 20, 1981, the American hostages were freed after 444 days in captivity.

The Reagans were well liked by a majority of the American people when they moved into the White House, and that feeling remained fairly steady for eight years. However, as First Lady, Nancy drew criticism for spending too much on new White House china while her husband was calling for cutbacks in domestic programs. *Time* magazine criticized her for wearing expensive gowns. White House chief of staff Donald Regan said she got an astrologer to set up the President's daily schedule. The First Lady did exert considerable influence on her husband, but she weathered the criticism and led a national campaign against drug abuse, called "Just Say No."

Ronald Reagan was the oldest President in U.S. history. When he left office in 1989, he was nearly 78 years old. Yet, despite his age, for most of his time in the White House, he was a remarkably fit and trim figure. (There was constant speculation in the press, however, about the fact that his hair never turned gray!) Unfortunately for him, Reagan had to prove his fitness soon after taking office. On the afternoon of March 30, 1981, he was very nearly assassinated. As the President, his aides, and guards left the Hilton Hotel in Washington, D.C., and headed for his limousine, a 25-year-old drifter fired six rounds from a .22 revolver. A policeman and a secret service agent were seriously wounded. Reagan's press secretary, James Brady, was shot in the head and still remains disabled today. Reagan very nearly died. A bullet punctured his lung and lodged close to his heart. At the sound of gunfire, the secret service guards had shoved the President through the open door of his limo and then fell on him. But they didn't realize he had been hit. When he began coughing up bright red blood, however, they rushed him to George Washington University Hospital. Two hours of surgery removed the bullet and repaired the lung. Doctors said he would have died had treatment been delayed only another five minutes. Said Reagan to the First Lady when he came out of surgery, "I forgot to duck." In 12 days he was back in the White House.

The would-be assassin was John W. Hinckley, son of a wealthy Colorado family. At his trial he pleaded not guilty by reason of insanity. He apparently shot Reagan to impress film actress Jodie Foster. Hinckley was committed to a mental institution in the nation's capital. He is still there.

The foundation of Reagan's administration was a revival of supply-side economics, which now came to be known as Reaganomics. According to this theory, if taxes are cut, people will be encouraged to spend more, which will increase and strengthen the country's economic growth. There will be more jobs, higher productivity, and more revenue for the government. This higher revenue in combination with government spending cuts will ultimately curb inflation and balance the budget.

Supply-side economics is also known as trickle-down economics. The idea is that the wealthy will invest more money, which will encourage more business, which will provide more jobs, which will ultimately reach those in the lowest economic levels. Trouble is, like many a theory, it looks good on paper, but watch out for the bugs when it's put into practice!

One problem is that when wealthy people have more money to spend, they might buy a million-dollar yacht instead of investing in a business. The new yacht may employ a few people for a while and make the yacht company richer, but it doesn't do much for the economy as a whole. And it certainly doesn't trickle down. Reagan's record on Reaganomics was mixed at best. Federal taxes were cut, but state taxes rose to restore some of the services. Reagan brought down the inflation rate, which is the rise in the general price of goods and services. But high interest rates, the amount charged to borrow money, brought on a severe depression in the economy. He was able to lower the unemployment rate to its lowest in the country's history. But the worst problem was the budget. Although the President called for a balanced budget amendment, he never submitted a balanced budget himself. The ideal for a government, just like an individual, is to have a balanced budget—that is, not to spend more than is taken in. It's not always easy to do. And when the government does spend more than it takes in, it must borrow money, usually in the form of government bonds. This borrowed money is the so-called national debt. In 1981, the total debt was nearly one trillion dollars. By the time Reagan left office, it had more than doubled. By the mid-1990s, the national debt had risen to almost five trillion dollars.

Part of the reason that Reagan could never balance the budget was a substantial increase in military spending. He began the largest U.S. peacetime military buildup in the nation's history. In 1983, he proposed the Strategic Defense Initiative, or SDI, which immediately became known as Star Wars after the 1977 popular film about interplanetary war. SDI was proposed as a defensive system, based in space, to protect the United States from attack by intercepting missiles in flight. Congress approved the initial funding for the project, but the enormous costs and doubts about how the plan would work brought on a storm of protest around the country.

The President did have most of the country's backing, however, for his strong anticommunist stand. And in this area, he got the nation into war—sort of—and peace—sort of. The war was actually an invasion of the smallest country in the Western Hemisphere, the tiny West Indies island state of Grenada. Americans were somewhat startled, in October 1983, to learn that U.S. troops had invaded the island, apparently with the support of the residents! The aim was to throw out the leftist government supported by Communist Cuba and rescue a few hundred Americans, mostly medical students. The invasion was successful on both counts, and the troops were home by Christmas, as Reagan promised.

The peace process concerned the Soviet Union, which Reagan had called "the focus of evil in the modern world." The relationship went downhill from there in 1983 when the Soviets shot down a South Korean airliner that had strayed into Soviet air space. All passengers and crew were killed, including an American congressman. But in 1985, Mikhail Gorbachev became

As early as October 31, 1983, US Marines were pulling out of Grenada in the Caribbean, after their successful invasion of the island.

the new Soviet leader anxious to forge a spirit of openness, or *glasnost*. So, in the strange-as-it-may-seem category, Reagan the staunch anticommunist signed the Intermediate Range Nuclear Forces (INF) Treaty with the Soviet Union in 1988. Under the agreement, both sides destroyed hundreds of medium- and short-range missiles. The world suddenly seemed a bit safer.

Ronald Reagan was not quite so successful with peace in other areas, however. After President Carter's trouble with the hostages in Iran, Reagan had promised, in his campaign speeches of 1980, to deal swiftly and harshly with international terrorism. Indeed, within days of becoming President he suspended all U.S. aid to the South American country of Nicaragua. His administration claimed that Nicaragua was aiding the Communist guerrillas in El Salvador. But keeping the lid on international problems was difficult as Americans around the globe found themselves victims of terrorism.

Among other violent incidents, U.S. citizens were killed by terrorists in Beirut, Lebanon (1983), aboard the Italian cruise ship *Achille Lauro* (1985), and in a West Berlin disco (1986). The most

Wreckage from Pan Am flight 103 and houses hit by the plane is strewn over the backyards of several homes in Lockerbie, Scotland, after the 747 crash on December 21, 1988.

horrendous incident occurred in December 1988 when a terrorist bomb sent a Pan Am jet crashing down on Lockerbie, Scotland, killing 259 on board and several on the ground. Reagan cited Libya's leader, Muammar al-Qaddafi, as the principal terrorist, calling him a "barbarian." He expelled Libyan diplomats from the United States and banned all trade with that country. In retaliation for the West Berlin bombing, which killed 61 Americans, Reagan sent F-111 fighter planes to bomb Libya's capital city of Tripoli. Supposedly, they hit Qaddafi's home and killed his adopted daughter. Some countries called this U.S. terrorism, but Reagan ignored the criticism.

Through much of this international turmoil, the President faced reelection in 1984. Dependable George Bush was once again his running mate. The Democratic opponents were Walter Mondale of Minnesota and Geraldine Ferraro of New York, the first woman on a major party ticket.

Mondale and Ferraro didn't have a chance. They were facing the Great Communicator. It didn't seem to matter to the public that the budget deficit was growing by leaps and bounds, that the wealth of the middle class was shrinking, and the wealth of the wealthy was growing. It didn't seem to matter that—at the time —there was no treaty on limiting nuclear arms with the Soviets, or that the costs of the U.S. military buildup were staggering. As with Ike in the 1950s, Americans in the 1980s just seemed to like Ronnie.

His age, of course, could have been an issue. Reagan, on his way to becoming the country's oldest President, was obviously starting to show some signs of wear. He stumbled over speech lines here and there, sometimes seemed a tad forgetful. But the old showman even managed to turn that into a plus. On his second televised debate with opponent Mondale, who was then 56 years old to Reagan's 73, the President said, "I am not going to exploit for political purposes my opponent's youth and inexperience." Even Mondale laughed.

Christa McAuliffe posed for this official NASA photograph a few months before the fateful Challenger *explosion in January 1986, in which she was killed.*

He didn't laugh on Election Day, however. Ronald Reagan swept back into office with 525 electoral votes to Mondale's 13. Fifty-nine percent of the popular votes went to the President.

Early in Reagan's second administration, on January 28, 1986, the nation suffered the worst disaster in the history of the U.S. space program. All seven astronauts, including the first private American citizen in space—schoolteacher Christa McAuliffe—were killed when the space shuttle *Challenger* exploded just seconds into the flight. The President spoke at a memorial service for the crew four days after the tragedy.

Later that year, Reagan's popularity took a slight dip. The public learned that members of his administration had secretly shipped arms to Iran, which was at war with Iraq at the time. In exchange, Iran was to use its influence to free American hostages being held in Beirut, Lebanon. The main trouble with all this was that it was Ronald Reagan who had repeatedly said that never, never would his administration negotiate with terrorists or make concessions to them. Then, it was disclosed that some of the money from the arms deal with Iran had been illegally used against the Communist government in Nicaragua.

A congressional committee began to look into the matter in mid-1987. For a time, Americans feared it was "Watergate all over again." Not quite. Some White House aides and officials were charged with destroying documents and failing to notify Congress of secret dealings. However, the committee decided that the President was not aware of where the money from the arms sale had gone. Yet, it criticized Reagan's "hands off" management style of government, which was said to be at least partly to blame for the mess. This was the lowest point in the President's popularity while in the White House.

Yet, in a way this was another example of what critics have called the "Teflon Presidency." Teflon is the brand name of a modern-age substance used to coat, among other things, frying pans, because nothing ever sticks to it. And so it seemed with President Ronald Reagan. No matter what potentially harmful rumor surfaced during his years in office, no matter what scandal cropped up, blame never stuck to Reagan. If he was asked about a questionable action on his part or that of someone in his administration, the President smiled his amiable smile, denied any knowledge, and the public by and large believed him. Critics charged throughout his eight years in office that he was a "hands-off" President, meaning that he delegated authority and work to others while he sat back. The public didn't blame him for that either. Teflon or not, Reagan had a curious and enduring love affair with much of the American public.

Some of Reagan's personal success in office, at least regarding his vote-getting ability, may have been due to the change in American politics that occurred during his presidency. Traditionally, the Republican party has always been smaller in number, in terms of registered voters, than the Democratic party. For a Republican to win office, therefore, it is necessary for the candidate to attract Democrats or those who consider themselves independent, belonging to neither party. Just as Franklin Roosevelt reformed the Democratic party in the 1930s, so Ronald Reagan reformed the Republican party in the 1980s. A new surge of religious conservatism, interest in smaller and more efficient government, and talk of taking power away from the central government in Washington and giving it to the state governments all attracted a "new Republican." Without new Republicans, Reagan could never have won the White House.

There was more trouble concerning Iran during Reagan's last two years in office. In early 1987, with Iran and Iraq at war in the Middle East, the Persian Gulf country of Kuwait asked for protection. Reagan agreed to have U.S. ships escort Kuwaiti vessels through the dangerous Persian Gulf. In May, Iraq fired on the U.S. frigate *Stark*. Thirty-seven sailors died. In October, an Iranian missile wounded 18 U.S. sailors. In return, U.S. missiles destroyed Iranian oil platforms in the Gulf. After some direct fighting between the two sides, a U.S. ship shot down an Iranian jetliner in July, killing 290 civilians. The Americans said the plane had been mistaken for a military fighter.

Despite his troubles overseas, when Reagan left office in 1989, he was on top again with the public. Ronald Reagan was surely the most popular retiring President since Dwight Eisenhower. The Reagans left the White House for Bel Air, California, where he planned to write his memoirs. In 1985, the President had recovered well from a colon cancer operation, but in retirement, his health seemed noticeably to decline. Then, in

Former Soviet President Mikhail Gorbachev visits former U.S. President Ronald Reagan at the latter's ranch in Santa Barbara in May 1993. Reagan has just given Gorbachev the cowboy hat he is wearing.

1995, a saddened Nancy Reagan announced that he was in the early stages of Alzheimer's disease. This is a wasting away of the brain cells, eventually causing memory loss and senility.

For all his popularity, Ronald Reagan as President has always been a controversial figure. He seems to inspire total love or hate, worship or disdain. Surprisingly perhaps, Democratic Senator Ted Kennedy said of Reagan in 1986, "He has contributed a spirit of good will and grace to the presidency." More expected was Libyan leader Qaddafi's comment, "Reagan embodies nothing more than the peak of a capitalist rotten society..." Cuba's Fidel Castro, another Reagan foe, was even more blunt. Said Castro, " He's a madman, an imbecile, and a bum." Former prime minister of Great Britain, Margaret Thatcher, had kinder words: "He has left America stronger, prouder, greater than ever before and we thank him for it."

Love him or hate him, respect him or scorn him, friend and foe alike admit that you always knew where you stood with Ronald Reagan. There were few mysteries in the Reagan White House. Now the Great Communicator is in retirement and facing his most severe personal challenge. But he has faced them before, and perhaps, with the aid of medical science, there will be at least one more win for the Gipper.

Names in the News in Reagan's Time

James Brady (1940–):

Illinois-born press secretary to Reagan, severely injured during Reagan assassination attempt in 1981. Sponsor of the Brady Bill to limit gun possession, passed in 1995.

Geraldine Ferraro (1935–):

New York politician and first woman to receive nomination of major political party for vice president (1984). Nominated by Clinton in 1993 as U.S. representative to the UN Human Rights Commission with rank of ambassador.

Alexander M. Haig, Jr. (1924—):

Pennsylvania-born secretary of state for Reagan. Drew public criticism after the President was shot, because he declared himself "in control of the government," which he was not.

William Holden (1918–1981):

Born William Franklin Beedle, Jr., in Illinois. Served as best man at Reagan's 1952 marriage to Nancy Davis. Longtime Hollywood leading man, winning an Oscar for *Stalag 17* (1953).

Sandra Day O'Connor (1930–):

Texas-born lawyer and judge. First woman to serve on the U.S. Supreme Court, nominated by Reagan (1981).

Geraldine Ferraro, with George Bush in the background, was the principal subject of this caricature by Robert Grossman.

Chapter Five

Bush: A Long Wait for a Short Term

George Herbert Walker Bush
(1989-1993)

Quite a few Presidents have served in the military. Several have been war heroes. But George Bush has a special distinction. At the age of 19, in 1943, he became the youngest pilot in the entire United States Navy! With World War II in full swing, he and his brand-new wings were sent to the South Pacific. On September 2, 1944, three months past his twentieth birthday, his three-man, single-engine Grumman Avenger was hit by antiaircraft fire. With his tailgunner already dead, Bush ordered his radioman to bail out, which he did but was killed in the fall. When Bush jumped, he slammed into the tail of the plane, tearing his chute and slicing open his scalp. However, he splashed down safely in the water. He spent some three hours in his yellow raft trying to stop the bleeding from his wound until he was rescued by the submarine *Finback*. For this mission, Bush won the Distinguished Flying Cross. His war duty left him slightly hard of hearing.

From war hero to President took 45 years. For eight of those years, he served as a steady backdrop to the popular, charismatic Ronald Reagan. Always in Reagan's shadow, to some extent even in the White House, he was never merely an appendage of Reagan's. He may have ridden into office on Reagan's coattails, but Bush was his own man. Although warm and friendly as Reagan, Bush has a quieter, more reserved personality. He is more at home in small groups than before large audiences. But make no mistake. George Bush is a tenacious campaigner, a man who knows what he wants, hangs on, and goes after it. All during his political career, he was touted as the ultimate party man, the loyal worker who could always be counted on. And he was. For his reward, Bush moved into the White House. To his bitter disappointment, the lease lasted only four years.

The second of five children, George Herbert Walker Bush was born on June 12, 1924, into a family of wealth and privilege. His maternal grandfather, George Herbert Walker, for whom he was named, was an investment banker. His father, Prescott S. Bush, was a businessman and senator from Connecticut. He did not live to see the most famous of his children become President. Bush's mother, Dorothy Walker Bush, did see her son in the White House. She was a strict disciplinarian who was determined that her children would not be spoiled by the wealth around them. She was also an outstanding athlete in baseball, basketball, track, and tennis. According to the story, when she was practically on the way to the hospital for the birth of her first child, she stopped long enough to smack a home run in the family softball game.

George was born in Milton, Massachusetts, but the family moved to Greenwich, Connecticut, a wealthy New York City suburb, when he was still an infant. When he was old enough to date, a chauffeur drove him and the young lady to their destination. His best childhood memories are the times spent at his grandmother's ocean estate in Kennebunkport, Maine. During his four years in office, the rambling home on Walker's Point became the summer White House.

If genes will get you to 1600 Pennsylvania Avenue, young George was a shoo-in. He is distantly related to Presidents Pierce, Lincoln, Theodore Roosevelt, and Ford, and Great Britain's Winston Churchill was his eighth cousin. For a dash of glamour, Marilyn Monroe was his ninth cousin.

Although he was a pudgy youngster, George grew tall, lean, and athletic. He is a fierce competitor who still doesn't like to lose. The former President is left-handed, six feet two, and has blue eyes and brown, now gray-streaked straight hair.

After Country Day School in Greenwich and prep school at Phillips Academy in Andover, Massachusetts, young George did just what he was advised not to do. Instead of going to college, he enlisted in the military, as did so many other young Americans during those early days of World War II. He joined the navy as a seaman second class but qualified for flight school.

By the time that Bush left the navy and headed for Yale University, he was a married man. On January 6, 1945, Lieutenant Junior Grade George Bush, now 20, married 19 year-old Barbara Pierce of Rye, New York. They had met at a Christmas dance three years earlier. They both admit that it was love at first sight. Barbara said he was the first boy she ever kissed. He named his bomber plane "Barbara."

Also from a well-to-do family, Barbara left Smith College after her marriage to follow her husband. What with his military, business, and political career, the Bushes would have 29 different homes in 17 different cities—the most prestigious, of course, being the White House. They were in California in 1949 when Barbara received news of a terrible tragedy. Her father had been driving to the train station one morning, his wife in the passenger seat and a cup of coffee between them. When the coffee started to spill, Marvin Pierce lunged for it and lost control of the car. His wife, Barbara's mother, was killed. The china coffee cup was unbroken.

George and Barbara Bush would eventually have six children. George W. is governor of Texas. Daughter Robin died of leukemia at the age of four, the most difficult time of the Bushes' long and happy marriage. John, called Jeb, is a banker and politician who narrowly lost the bid for the Florida governorship in 1994. Neil is an oilman in Denver, Colorado, and Marvin a businessman in Virginia. The youngest is Dorothy, or Doro,

George and Barbara Bush posed for this photo with their children (clockwise from left) Neil, John, George, Marvin, and Dorothy in 1964 when he first ran for the U.S. Senate.

a businesswoman in Washington, D.C. The Bush family is close and George and Barbara delight in their several grandchildren.

After graduating from Yale with honors in 1948, Bush decided on a career in oil. He worked in Texas and California, becoming successful but increasingly bored. For some time he had been active in Texas Republican politics, so in 1964 he decided to run for a U.S. Senate seat. He lost. But in 1966, after selling his oil interests for $1 million, he was elected to the House of Representatives and reelected in 1968. A conservative in money matters, he voted for the Civil Rights Act that year.

In 1970, a second try for a Senate seat from Texas also ended in defeat. This so discouraged Bush that he almost gave up politics. But Richard Nixon, then in office, hadn't forgotten him. It was Nixon who had urged the loyal Republican from Texas to give up his safe House seat for a run at the Senate. His reward was the post of ambassador to the United Nations (1971–73).

Bush spent a lot of time at the United Nations pushing for a "two China" policy, which failed in the end. It would have admitted mainland China to the UN while allowing Taiwan, whose government had been ousted from China when the Communists took over, to keep a seat. Eventually, China was in and Taiwan was out.

Nixon was reelected in 1972 and Bush wanted a new job. What he didn't want was to be chairman of the Republican party. But the President requested, and Bush was, after all, a party man. He spent the rest of Nixon's administration trying to defend the battered President against Watergate charges. Bush was among the last of his supporters to desert him. However, even loyal Bush finally could see no way out and urged the President to resign.

Once more, George Bush was looking for a job. What he really wanted was to be vice president. Gerald Ford, who took over from Nixon, instead chose New York governor Nelson Rockefeller. But, he did offer Bush whatever ambassadorship he wished. Bush chose China in 1974. Because relations between China and the United States did not yet permit the exchange of ambassadors, Bush's official title was chief of the U.S. Liaison Office.

Bush was happy in China, but duty called once again. Ford asked him to take over the directorship of the Central Intelligence Agency (CIA). The CIA was generally regarded as a graveyard for someone with higher political ambitions. However, as before, he couldn't refuse.

George Bush was the first politician to head the CIA and generally performed well in this sensitive post. In fact, he bent over backward not to favor either Republicans or Democrats. Morale at the intelligence agency had seriously declined in the past few years because of secret plots against foreign leaders and other

Bush is accompanied to the Beijing Airport in China in December 1975 by Lin Ping, an official of the People's Republic of China, after the future President was recalled to Washington to become head of the CIA.

such covert activity. Bush worked hard to restore both the morale and the image of the CIA, and when he left in 1977, even the Democrats said he had been one of the best in the job. Actually, Bush would have liked to have stayed there. But politics is politics and the new President—Democrat Jimmy Carter—wanted his own man.

Out of work again, where was George Bush to go? Why not the top? He decided to campaign for the 1980 Republican presidential nomination. Unfortunately, Ronald Reagan decided the same thing. At first, it appeared that Bush would be a formidable rival. He came out first in the Iowa primary election in January 1980, calling Reagan's theory of trickle-down economics "voodoo economics." But by May it was clear that Bush would be second best once again. So, loyal Bush graciously withdrew and urged Republicans to support Reagan.

At the Republican National Convention in Detroit that July, Reagan got in on the first ballot, with 13 votes cast for Bush. A strong behind-the-scenes cry went up for Reagan to nominate former President Gerald Ford as his running mate. But when no deal with Ford could be made, the vice presidential spot went to George Herbert Walker Bush.

Bush was a busy vice president over the next eight years, mostly traveling to foreign countries. He rarely spoke up at Cabinet meetings and generally maintained a low profile. So low that UN Ambassador Jeane J. Kirkpatrick once said she had no idea where the vice president stood on most foreign policy issues. The years of standing behind Reagan generally reinforced Bush's image as a steadfast, dependable, solid party man, someone who could be counted on.

When an assassination attempt put President Reagan in the hospital, Bush presided over Cabinet meetings. When a cancer operation had Reagan under anesthesia for eight hours, presidential powers were transferred to Bush under the Twenty-Fifth Amendment to the Constitution. During the Iran arms trouble,

Bush claimed that he had no knowledge of the secret arms deal information, and nothing was ever proven.

Then, it was 1988—at last. Finally, after years of loyal and hard work, it was time for George Bush to step into the spotlight. The Republican convention in New Orleans that August was not without controversy, however. Most of the furor erupted over Bush's choice of a running mate, Senator Dan Quayle of Indiana. Even loyal Bush supporters were at a loss to explain why he would select an obviously ill-prepared junior senator for the number two spot. Indeed, why? Although the press speculated that Bush did not want someone who would overshadow him— and Quayle certainly qualified on that score—the real reasons for the choice were never specified.

So began the unforgettable presidential election campaign of 1988. It was unforgettable chiefly because it was the most negative campaign in anyone's memory. The Democratic opponents were Michael S. Dukakis, little-known governor of Massachusetts, and his running mate, Senator Lloyd Bentsen of Texas. Bush, who presented himself at the convention as a quiet, dedicated civil servant who wanted a "quieter and gentler nation," brought out the more strident side of his nature in his slashing attacks on his opponent. In fact, both candidates spent far more time bashing each other than talking about issues.

Because, as governor, Dukakis had vetoed bills to require a daily pledge of allegiance to the flag in schools and because he opposed the death penalty, Bush implied that his opponent was unpatriotic and soft on crime. Dukakis wondered aloud how anyone who was a former director of the CIA could not know about drug smuggling in Panama, as Bush claimed.

Dukakis also wondered aloud how anyone could choose unqualified Dan Quayle as a running mate. Indeed, even after the election, Quayle was never able to live down that image. During Quayle's televised visit to a school, an 11-year-old boy wrote the word "potato" on the blackboard. Quayle lightly admonished the boy for spelling it incorrectly. The boy was right. Quayle was cited in the press for such gaffes which continued to support his perceived image as inexperienced.

Bush scored points during the campaign with his quip of "Read my lips, no new taxes!" But it is perhaps indicative of this campaign that one of its most memorable lines was delivered at the Democratic convention. Speaker Ann Richards, then Texas state treasurer, described wealthy but—to her—wimpy Bush as someone who "was born with a silver foot in his mouth."

Just 57 percent of an increasingly annoyed public showed up at the polls on Election Day. That was the lowest turnout since these figures were first noted in 1964. The campaign had been so negative that a large number of newspapers throughout the country refused to endorse either man. But when the votes were counted, Bush had won his turn in the White House, 426 electoral votes to 111 for Dukakis, 54 percent of the popular vote to 46 percent. Bush was helped by the highly visible campaigning of popular Ronald Reagan and by the fact that Dukakis himself was a poor campaigner.

The long years of party loyalty and playing second fiddle had paid off. In 1988, George Bush became the forty-first President of the United States. He was the first sitting vice president since Martin Van Buren (1837) to be elected President. He was the first President since William Howard Taft (1909) to win the White House but lose both houses of Congress (the Democrats took control of both the House and Senate). He was the first President since Herbert Hoover to follow a President of his own party who had retired.

George and Barbara Bush moved into the White House and tried to bring some calm to the frayed nerves of the nation. The First Lady helped. Friendly and unpretentious, Barbara Bush was a great change from the elegant style of Nancy Reagan. The new First Lady refused to dye her white hair and was as often photographed in baggy garden slacks as in the newest fashions.

She told newspeople that her pearls were fake and she wore them to cover wrinkles in her neck. Beneath the breeziness, however, Barbara Bush became a tireless worker for the cause of literacy in the United States.

This partly sprang from the fact that she had years before uncovered the dyslexia of son Neil. Dyslexia is a disorder that inhibits the ability to read or spell in an otherwise normally intelligent person. A dyslexic person might, for instance, see the letter "b" as a "d," so that the word big is read as dig. The earlier the disorder is recognized, the quicker treatment can start and the more likely the disability can be overcome.

First Lady Barbara Bush reads to children during a visit in January 1990 to the National Learning Center at the Capitol Children's Museum.

George Bush as President made no drastic departures from the policies of Ronald Reagan as President, although Bush is not as conservative. However, the economy worsened and unemployment rose. In a lingering recession, more businesses failed than at any time since the 1930s and fewer jobs were created. The budget deficit doubled to some $350 billion. In addition, Bush agreed to tax hikes. Where was the campaign pledge of "Read my lips, no new taxes"? That would come back to haunt him.

In 1989, Bush bailed out hundreds of savings and loan banks. These are financial institutions that take in savings from the public and invest them mostly in home mortgages. The banks had gone under due to corruption or mismanagement. Bush's action was met with some skepticism in the press since son Neil was a director of a Denver, Colorado, savings and loan. The bank had gone under with a cost of $1 billion to the taxpayers.

For some time, the United States had been aware that the leader of Panama, General Manuel Antonio Noriega, was involved in drug trafficking. He was indicted on drug charges in Florida. The U.S. government imposed sanctions—limiting or stopping the sale of goods—against Panama, but nothing ousted Noriega. Then, in late 1989, some Panamanian officers tried to overthrow him. Bush refused U.S. help, which seemed to indicate that the President did not want war under any circumstances. But that December, an American marine was shot by Panamanian troops, and Bush sent in U.S. forces. Most nations around the world condemned the United States, but most Panamanians welcomed the troops. After four days of fighting, in which 23 Americans were killed, it was learned that Noriega had taken refuge inside the Vatican mission. He surrendered in January, was tried on drug charges in Florida, and sentenced to 40 years in prison. During the invasion, for the first time in American history, a woman, Captain Linda Bray, led U.S. troops in combat.

With Reagan in the White House, the United States had tried in various ways to topple the Communist government in Nicaragua. Bush abandoned that policy, admitting it had failed. But in early 1990, to almost everyone's surprise, the widow of a crusading newspaper publisher, Violeta Chamorro, won the presidency of Nicaragua and threw out the Communist government. Bush immediately promised U.S. aid and lifted the economic restraints that had been placed against Nicaragua.

Two dramatic historical events took place during the Bush years, one not of his doing, the other at his order. The first was the surprising collapse of the Communist world. Since the end of World War II, the United States had been struggling with the threat of Communist world domination. But now, in the late 1980s, communism seemed to collapse of its own accord. In June 1989, Poland voted in the first noncommunist government since World War II. An electrician named Lech Walesa was later elected President. Communist East Germany and democratic West Germany, divided since World War II, became one—noncommunist—nation in October 1990. Other countries threw

A demonstrator takes a sledgehammer to the Berlin Wall at the Brandenburg Gate on November 11, 1989, as East German border guards look on from above.

off communism as well, but nothing was so astounding as its fall in the Soviet Union itself.

In 1990, the monopoly of the Communist party was repealed. President Mikhail Gorbachev emerged as a new kind of Soviet leader. He was willing to grant the various Soviet republics more freedom. But in late 1991, the hardliners—those who stuck to the Communist doctrine—tried to depose him. He was saved with the help of the president of the Russian Republic, Boris Yeltsin. It was too little, too late. The Soviet Union disintegrated into separate republics. Gorbachev resigned from a country that no longer existed. Economic chaos has since threatened the existence of all the republics that formerly made up the Soviet Union.

The second dramatic event of the Bush administration was the Persian Gulf War, August 2, 1990, to April 3, 1991. It was prompted by Iraq's invasion of Kuwait, the oil-rich emirate in the Persian Gulf. The United Nations ordered Iraq to get out. Iraqi President Saddam Hussein paid no attention. On January 17, 1991, President Bush ordered Allied troops to invade under Operation Desert Shield, later Operation Desert Storm, led by U.S. Army General H. Norman Schwarzkopf.

In 100 hours of combat, Kuwait was liberated and Iraq forced out. The United States had sent more than 500,000 troops, of whom 148 were killed, including the first U.S. military women lost in combat. Iraq tried an interesting if useless attempt at

Before quitting Kuwait, Iraqi troops set fire to the oil fields, destroying or damaging all 950 oil wells. Daily, more than four million barrels of oil went up in flames.

psychological warfare during Operation Desert Storm. A radio broadcast to the U.S. military warned that while a soldier was fighting, Robert Redford back home was dating his girlfriend!

Despite the defeat and economic sanctions, Iraq's Hussein remained in power. Even so, Bush's approval rating jumped to 89 percent after the Persian Gulf War. One might have thought that fact alone would put him back in the White House. But, when the fighting died down, the poor economy reared its ugly head. And that concerned voters more than pride in the military. Bush faced an unknown—Bill Clinton of Arkansas. But he also faced a strong independent candidate, the unpredictable and feisty Ross Perot, a Texas billionaire who opposed both candidates. His blunt, folksy speech amused some and attracted others. And even though he withdrew from the race before Election Day, he garnered some 19 percent of the votes.

Campaigning for signatures to place him on the ballot, Ross Perot speaks to a rally at the Capitol in Frankfort, Kentucky. Perot volunteers later handed over more than 40,000 signatures to have his name put on the ballot for the Kentucky primary.

Bush was not helped either by the hardline conservative tone of the Republican National Convention. Ultraconservative Pat Buchanan delivered a speech that was critical of everything and everyone not in the conservative Republican camp. Bill Clinton's wife, Hillary, was denounced for "radical feminism." A speech delivered by the vice president's wife, Marilyn Quayle, implied that all mothers who worked outside the home were somehow shameful. Senator John Danforth of Missouri, a moderate Republican, called the convention "a total disaster."

It certainly was for George Bush. Behind in the polls from the very beginning, he narrowed the gap between himself and Clinton but never caught up. Bill Clinton toppled the incumbent President with an electoral count of 370 to 168. Bush was devastated by the outcome. He and Barbara went to Texas and retirement, after spending a career pursuing a very short dream.

George Bush is a hard man to comprehend. He says of himself, "I'm a conservative, but I'm not a nut about it." Behind the warm smile and impeccable manners is a driven political animal who strives to win and will never give up. Engaging and witty, he is tenacious in his pursuit of a goal. His critics say his main failure as President was his inability to explain and interpret his decisions to the American public. As Robert Straus, former chairman of the Democratic party once said, "George is a darn good guy, but he just doesn't come through well."

Names in the News in Bush's Time

Mario Cuomo (1932–):

New York-born governor of New York (1983–1994). Eloquent speaker. Considered running for Democratic nomination that would oppose Bush in 1994, but declined.

Elizabeth H. Dole (1936–):

Secretary of labor (1989–1990), transportation secretary in Reagan administration. Married to Robert Dole, long-time senator and Republican candidate for President (1996). Now head of the American Red Cross.

Colin Powell (1937–):

New York-born general; first African American chairman of the Joint Chiefs of Staff (1989). Held overall responsibility for U.S. military in Operations Desert Shield and Desert Storm against Iraq (1990–1991). Urged to join Robert Dole on Republican ticket for 1996 election, but declined.

Mario Cuomo, the avenging warrior, was depicted astride the Democratic donkey, in this 1988 cartoon by Robert Grossman. Cuomo was riding high in popularity polls prior to his 1992 reelection as New York's governor.

Chapter Six

Bill Clinton, Dark Horse from Arkansas

William Jefferson Clinton
(1993-2001)

*I*n 1992, he was a little-known governor from the state of Arkansas. Yet, he beat a sitting President in the race for the White House. In 1996, he himself was a sitting President who most people said lacked character and consistency. Yet, he beat a well-known and longtime senator to renew his lease in the White House. An apparent miracle man, his rise to the top began in very modest circumstances with a very troubled childhood. He is William Jefferson Clinton of Hope, Arkansas, forty-second President of the United States and a true American success story.

If you're looking for Hope, you better have a big map. It is tucked away in the southwestern corner of Arkansas about 32 miles northeast of Texarkana, twin cities on the Texas borderline. Clinton was born there on August 19, 1946, and christened William Jefferson Blythe the Fourth. His father, a traveling salesman, was killed in an auto accident shortly before his birth. Clinton later said it was his father's early death, at age 29, that made him determined to achieve quick success. "Most kids don't think about when they might die," he said, "but I thought about it all the time."

His father's sudden death left his mother, Virginia Cassidy Blythe, with no way to support herself and her infant son. So, baby Bill stayed with her parents while she went to New Orleans for a year to study to be a nurse-anesthetist. When Bill was four, his mother married Roger Clinton, an auto dealer, and the family moved to Hot Springs. It was not a happy move because it was not a happy marriage. Clinton was an abusive alcoholic who beat his wife and once fired a gun at her. Luckily for Bill's mother, the bullet hit the wall instead of her. Such episodes led to calls to the police and finally to a divorce in 1962. However, they remarried in three months, over the boy's strong objections. Roger junior was born when Bill was ten, and Bill frequently defended his younger half brother against abuse. Finally, when Bill was 14, he found the physical and moral courage to stand up to his stepfather, warning him never again to hurt his mother. From that incident grew Clinton's strong feelings against any kind of physical violence. "It's a really painful thing to threaten to beat up your stepfather," he said later.

The beatings stopped but the unhappy marriage continued. At the age of 16, Bill legally changed his name to Clinton in hopes of cementing family ties. His stepfather finally stopped drinking when Bill was in college and the two made their peace with each other before the elder Clinton died of cancer in 1967. Virginia Clinton would remarry twice more and remain a staunch supporter of her son until her death in 1994. President Clinton said of his mother, "She always worked, did a good job as a parent; we had a lot of adversity in our life when I was growing up, and she handled it real well."

Despite the troubled atmosphere at home, young Clinton was a fine student. His intelligence and drive were obvious at an early age. However, he did get a D in conduct in the second grade for shouting out the answers before anyone else had a chance. At Hot Springs High School, besides getting good grades, he found time to play tenor sax in a jazz combo with two other boys. They wore sunglasses and called themselves the Three Blind Mice. He also worked as a volunteer in nonprofit organizations. A classmate later recalled that Bill Clinton was very friendly and always "running for something."

Future President Bill Clinton of Arkansas shakes hands with then President John F. Kennedy at the 1963 meeting of the American Legion Boys Nation convention in Washington, D.C.

Perhaps that led to his choice of politics as a career. Perhaps it was his meeting with John F. Kennedy in 1963, just before the President was assassinated in Dallas, Texas. Clinton was in Washington, D.C., as a member of Boys' State, a leadership group affiliated with the American Legion and made up of students with strong political interests. He toured the White House and shook the President's hand. Then, he went back to Arkansas and decided to become a politician.

After he graduated from Hot Springs High School in 1964—fourth in a class of 323, Clinton spent the summer working for Senator J. William Fulbright of Arkansas. He got the job when he replied to an offer of part-time work for $3,000 annually, or a full time job for $5,000 annually. Clinton said he'd take two part-time jobs! He got the job on his qualifications, not his humor, but in politics as anything else, humor never hurts.

Having decided to study foreign relations, Clinton enrolled at Georgetown University in the nation's capital. He was class president for two years and volunteered to help workers who tried to clean up the city following riots in Washington after civil rights leader Martin Luther King, Jr., was assassinated in 1968. By the time he graduated that same year, the United States was deeply involved in war in Vietnam. The country was divided on American participation, which Clinton opposed. Undoubtedly, he was influenced by the views of Senator Fulbright, who was a leading critic of the Vietnam War.

Having won a Rhodes scholarship, that October Bill Clinton sailed aboard the USS *United States* to England and Oxford University. Rhodes scholarships were established at Oxford in 1902 by Englishman Cecil John Rhodes (1853–1902), an empire builder in British South Africa. The scholarships were open to intelligent young men from the British colonies as well as the United States and Germany, with young women becoming eligible in 1975.

Once again, Clinton was a fine student. Yet, he found time to join public demonstrations against the war in Vietnam. During his first year at Oxford, Clinton received a deferment, an official postponement of military service, which kept him out of the army and Vietnam. At the end of his deferment, he was eligible for the draft but was never called. His antiwar stand and draft deferment status would draw sharp criticism from Republican opponents during the 1992 presidential campaign. So would his rather silly statement that he had tried marijuana at Oxford, but "didn't inhale."

In early 1970, Clinton traveled to the Soviet Union for a first-hand look at Russian life. Later that year, he left Oxford for what he regarded as bigger stakes. Yale University Law School had offered him a scholarship. (Oxford gave him an honorary doctorate in civil law in 1994.) To add to his meager funds, Clinton held part-time jobs and took out student loans, and, in 1973, he graduated from Yale with a degree in law.

After Yale, Clinton went back home. Although he taught at the University of Arkansas Law School, he was just biding time until he got a chance to run for public office. That happened in 1974 when he tried for a seat in the Arkansas congress and lost.

Although his political career wasn't doing so well, Clinton had better luck with his private life. On October 11, 1975, he married Hillary Rodham, another bright student whom he had met at Yale. She was a conservative Republican at the time. Born October 26, 1947, she was the daughter of a textile company owner in Illinois. Before attending Yale, she had graduated with honors from Wellesley College.

Clinton's political life improved as well when he became the state attorney general in 1976. His work earned him a place on the U.S. Junior Chamber of Commerce list of the Ten Outstanding Young Men in the country in 1978.

Bigger things were just around the corner for the ambitious man from Hope. Clinton won the race for governor of Arkansas in 1978, becoming—at age 32— the state's youngest governor ever and the nation's youngest in 40 years. The chairman of the Democratic party, John White, boasted that Clinton would be on the presidential ticket in ten years. White was wrong; it took 13 years.

Another White—Frank—made another boast concerning Clinton. This White, a Republican and a bank president, boasted that he would defeat the new governor after

During his term as governor of Arkansas, Bill Clinton and his wife, Hillary Rodham Clinton, arrive at the White House at the invitation of President and Mrs. Reagan to attend a dinner.

one term. White was right. Two things threw Bill Clinton out of office. One was his highly unpopular tax hike to finance a highway improvement program. The other was a Ronald Reagan sweep into the White House. When a President, or other political figure, is extremely popular with the people, as was Reagan, he or she is said to have "long coattails." This means that many other lesser candidates of the same party are swept into office as well. The popular Reagan's coattails threw Clinton out in 1980, making him, at age 34, the youngest ex-governor in U.S. history.

So, it was back to practicing law in Little Rock. This gave Clinton time to think about what went wrong. In 1982, he was back on the campaign trail telling voters to put his first term down to a "young man's mistake." They apparently believed him for he beat Frank White in 1984 to get back in the governor's mansion. He won reelection for a third term in 1988.

Clinton's toughest decision as governor involved his half brother. Roger Clinton was caught in a cocaine sting operation in 1984. The governor knew about the setup by police but allowed it to happen because he felt it would ultimately save the young man's life. Indeed, Roger now agrees with that decision and supports his half brother. The younger Clinton was sentenced to two years in prison and after his parole, the entire family, including the governor, underwent group counseling. Today, Roger Clinton is married and works in Hollywood as a television production assistant.

By the time Clinton finished his third term, he was named by *Newsweek* magazine as the most effective governor in the nation. His record rested mainly on education reform. His education package included the first competency test for teachers in the country. It was deeply criticized and resented at first, but Clinton stood firm. Eventually, many of his critics conceded that he raised the quality of education in the state—even though he raised the state sales tax to do it! When he got to the White House, Clinton continued to make education a prime concern.

In 1991, Governor Clinton announced that he would campaign for President of the United States on the Democratic ticket. Most Americans had no idea who he was. The press wrote him off early with three strikes. One: Republican President George Bush was basking in praise because of the successful outcome of the Persian Gulf War. Two: Opponents made much of Clinton's avoiding military service in Vietnam. He was branded a draft dodger. Three: Stories and rumors spread about Clinton's relationships with other women during his marriage, especially a supposedly long affair with a nightclub singer named Gennifer Flowers. Clinton denied the charges and appeared with Hillary on national television to deal with the issue.

For all his years in the White House, the issue of character and infidelity continued to dog Bill Clinton. But nothing has been proven and the rumors did not keep him from victory.

Despite all the charges and critics, Clinton won the Democratic nomination and chose Al Gore from Tennessee as his running mate. Clinton and Gore would become the youngest President/vice president team ever to win office.

At first glance, it looked like the post-Gulf War popularity of President Bush, Clinton's Republican opponent, would keep him in the White House. But underneath all the rah-rah patriotism, the American public was uneasy and growing testy about the country's longstanding economic decline. Things just didn't "feel right." And the Republicans did themselves,

As a presidential candidate in October 1992, Bill Clinton answers questions during a three-way televised debate while then-President George Bush and independent candidate Ross Perot listen.

and the President, no favor at their convention. Their biting criticism of Hillary Clinton disturbed many voters, as did an address by Marilyn Quayle, wife of the vice president. She seemed to imply that women who worked outside the home were somehow less valuable, and certainly less noble, than full-time homemakers. And a speech by Pat Buchanan, outspoken commentator for the conservative wing of the Republican party, only heightened what seemed to many viewers as politics at its nastiest. To moderate voters across the nation, the Republicans began to look ultra-ultra conservative.

Bill Clinton won the election with just 43 percent of the vote to Bush's 38 percent. Clinton was helped by the appearance of third party candidate Ross Perot, a billionaire and ex-IBM salesman from Texas who charmed many voters with his folksy speeches and reeled in 19 percent of the vote. The electoral vote count gave 370 to Clinton and 168 to Bush.

William Jefferson Clinton entered the White House as the youngest man to sit in the Oval Office since John F. Kennedy and the first of the post-World War II generation to be President. Hillary Rodham Clinton was the first lawyer to become First Lady. Chelsea, the Clinton's only child, became the first school-age youngster in the White House since Amy, daughter of President Jimmy and Rosalynn Carter, in 1977. Born in 1980, Chelsea is named for "Chelsea Morning," a song made popular by

After voting in the 1992 election, Hillary Clinton leaves the voting place with Chelsea, the Clinton's daughter, in hand.

folksinger Judy Collins. Chelsea is a bright student whom the Clintons have successfully sheltered from the glare of public life. She attended Sidwell Friends School in Washington, D.C., and was accepted at Stanford University in California for the fall 1997 semester. However, when she moved into the White House, even she took a backseat in the media to First Cat, Socks. He is a black and white domestic shorthair of uncertain ancestry who sometimes is seen searching in vain for mice on the manicured White House grounds. The President is allergic to Socks, but tolerates the First Cat by taking allergy shots.

Actually, Bill Clinton is allergic to just about everything except presidential campaigns. He can't tolerate dust, mold, pollen, Christmas trees, dairy products, and, of course, cats. He has chronic laryngitis and is slightly hard of hearing. He is tall— six feet two and a half inches —with thick, mostly gray hair and blue-gray eyes. A hearty eater, Clinton is sometimes inclined to put on a few too many pounds, which gives him the appearance of a chubby teddy bear despite his daily jogs.

Bill Clinton entered the White House with youth and drive and ambition, but quickly discovered that those assets don't necessarily make the job easier. He was immediately embroiled in domestic problems, such as economic recovery, health care reform, civil rights issues, anticrime measures, and even presidential appointments. Two days after his inauguration, his choice for attorney general, Zoe Baird, was withdrawn after it was learned that she had hired an illegal alien as domestic help. The press immediately called this "Nannygate," mimicking the Watergate scandal of the Nixon era. Clinton's second choice, Kimba Wood, had the same problem, but his third choice, Janet Reno, became the nation's first female attorney general. Critics said the President should have checked more thoroughly before naming his choice to fill the post.

But the domestic fiasco that really set the tone of Clinton's first administration concerned gays in the military. During the campaign, he had promised that the U.S. military would no longer discharge someone on the basis of homosexuality. Once in the White House, when he attempted to act on that promise, he met with a storm of protest from conservative voters. Clinton backed down and announced a new policy—"don't ask, don't tell." Liberal critics said he had no backbone and was wishy-washy, a charge that stuck. Conservatives felt he still went too far.

Not surprisingly, with so much of his attention at home, the President was criticized for not paying heed to foreign policy, especially as conflicts were breaking out in such places as Bosnia in Europe, Somalia and Rwanda in Africa, and Haiti in the Caribbean. However, he silenced his critics by various peace-making efforts during his administration. Among them was his involvement in bringing the leaders of Israel and the Arab nations to the peace table. Also, he dispatched former President Jimmy Carter and former Chief of Staff General Colin Powell to cool tempers in Haiti.

Even so, Clinton continued to be plagued with problems, small and large, that steadily eroded his already shaky approval rating. In April 1993, federal agents killed about 80 people after a standoff in Waco, Texas, by a religious cult known as Branch Davidians. Following a demand to surrender illegal firearms and an unsuccessful raid on the Davidian compound, during which four agents were killed, the standoff lasted 51 days. It ended on April 19 when tear gas was pumped into the compound. The loss of life caused critics to charge Attorney General Janet Reno with mishandling the affair.

In July, Clinton's deputy counsel at the White House, Vincent Foster, killed himself. He was part of the investigation that had begun on "Whitewater." This was a real estate venture in Arkansas in which the Clintons, then in the governor's mansion, were partners with banker James McDougal. The investigation sought to discover whether the Clintons had improperly used their influence to bring about the real estate deal. Although

Whitewater investigations continued throughout Clinton's terms and some friends and associates of the President were found guilty, no charges have been brought against the Clintons.

In late September, the President unveiled the health care reform plan, a centerpiece of his domestic policy. This probably caused the most stir of all. Both houses of Congress and most Americans agreed that something needed to be done about the already high and constantly rising costs of health care. The elderly were especially worried that their life savings would disappear if sickness hit them. Everyone wanted the government to do something. What Clinton did was to place his wife in charge of health care reform, but this move irked many Americans. To them, a First Lady was supposed to do the things that First Ladies usually did—host parties, look attractive, fight illiteracy, beautify parks, stay in the background. But Hillary Clinton was doing what she does best—being a lawyer. Even without the bias against the First Lady, the sweeping health care reform package might have died anyway, since there was opposition from many sides about its high cost. By mid-1994, the White House conceded that health care reform was dead for the time being.

Clinton had some success in September of that year when he sent U.S. troops into the Caribbean nation of Haiti to ensure a peaceful return of that country's elected president, Jean-Bertrand Aristide. November, however, was another discouraging time for the White House. In the off-year elections, which take place midway between presidential elections, the Republicans swept both houses of Congress for the first time in 40 years. People began talking about only four years in the White House for Bill Clinton.

And, indeed, things didn't seem to get much better. In a fight over who controlled government spending between the President and Congress, the U.S. government shut down twice, for six days in November and again in December 1995. This meant, among other things, that government offices closed and government workers weren't paid. Actually, this shutdown may have helped Clinton's reelection since it painted the radical members of the Republican party as mean and uncaring. However, disapproval of the First Lady's role in government grew stronger and louder. Investigations into Whitewater continued, egged on by a Republican opposition that was beginning to believe it could take over the White House again...and soon. References to past romantic entanglements by the President cropped up now and again. Practically everyone said he flip-flopped too much on the issues. It really looked like the forty-second President of the United States might be a short-termer.

But it's not for nothing that Bill Clinton has been called the "Comeback Kid"! Give him a political challenge and his eyes become sparklier, his step springier, his enthusiasm boundless once again. So, despite low favorable ratings by the American public, few were surprised when the White House announced that the President would seek a second term.

Suddenly, the lines around his eyes, put there by four years of turmoil and stress, seemed to disappear into the breadth of his smile. Bill Clinton on the campaign trail is a master.

Still, the pollsters—those people who try to discover how voters are feeling about candidates—didn't think it was going to be easy, at least not at the beginning. After a good deal of wrangling, the Republicans settled on their candidate—longtime senator and Clinton foe, Bob Dole of Kansas. A decorated veteran, his right arm disabled from a battle wound during World War II, Dole was an experienced campaigner. Yet, he tended to speak in half-sentences and as though he were reading an outline. According to close associates, he has a fine sense of humor, but it rarely showed on the campaign trail.

Clinton also had a little good luck on his side. Aggressive, seemingly mean-spirited attacks on all opposition by the Republican-controlled Congress were slowly antagonizing

Democrats and more moderate Republicans alike. The economy, although not robust, was doing well enough to keep Americans uneasy perhaps but not angry.

Both candidates vowed to keep the campaign on a slightly higher level than years before, with questionable results. In the end, the Comeback Kid came through again. When the votes were counted after the November 5, 1996, election, Bill Clinton was back in the White House for a second term, the first Democratic President to be reelected since Franklin D. Roosevelt in 1936!

Once again, Clinton did not get a majority of the popular vote, that is, at least 51 percent, but he beat Dole by more than 45 million to nearly 38 million. Perot was in the race again, getting no electoral votes but nearly 26 million popular votes. Dole took 159 electoral votes to Clinton's 379.

Is he really a miracle man? After all, William Jefferson Clinton is not regarded as a particularly popular President, although his ratings, especially after his second election, were sometimes quite high. No one extols his high moral character or his values. He is criticized for changing his mind, or not making up his mind. Opponents say he has no backbone. Even his friends readily admit he has flaws.

So why has he won election after election? If people don't like him so much or trust him so much, why do they vote for him? How come Bill Clinton got two terms in the White House when someone like George Bush, whose high moral character has rarely been challenged, could only get one?

His supporters say Clinton gets a bad press, meaning that newspapers and other media criticize him unfairly, and that people, underneath it all, realize he's really trying to make life better for Americans. Veterans of the political scene say that, sure, Clinton is morally flawed and may be even a slick politician, but then so is Bob Dole and most others in Congress, and Americans know that. So, why, they ask, pick on Clinton? At least he's trying.

Some blame the Congress for Clinton's second election. U.S. voters *like* having a President of one party and a Congress of the other. They think two strong parties protect citizens against too much power on any one side. Still others claim that times are pretty good economically for most Americans in the mid to late 1990s. Don't upset the apple cart; don't change.

In addition, despite the criticisms and flaws, Clinton as President also can point to accomplishments. In August 1993, he was able to get Congress to pass a deficit reduction plan that cuts federal spending and raises income taxes on the wealthy. Wanting to be known as the education President, he has expanded the Head Start program, which aids young children in low

With former White House press secretary James Brady looking on President Clinton signs the Brady Bill, restricting handgun sales, into law on November 30, 1993.

economic areas, and passed a Goals 2000 bill, which aims for a 90 percent high-school graduation rate of the nation's children by the beginning of the twenty-first century. His anticrime legislation mandates a waiting period for the purchase of handguns and authorizes money to hire new police officers and build more prisons. His administration has overcome great obstacles against barriers to international trade. After a long and bitter debate, the North American Free Trade Agreement (NAFTA) was signed in late 1993. It promotes free trade among Mexico, Canada, and the United States. Clinton also did what three Republican administrations before him had failed to do—overcame longstanding disputes about the amount of goods imported and exported between Japan and the United States. Late in Clinton's first administration, Japan agreed to open its domestic markets to foreign competition. He has supported reform toward a more democratic society in Russia and averted possible trouble by getting North Korea to agree to dismantle its nuclear development program.

In office, Bill Clinton has had ups and downs, successes and failures. Perhaps he has had something else as well. A song from the great musical *My Fair Lady* implies that some things, no matter how improbable, can be overcome with "just a little bit of luck." Surely, President William Jefferson Clinton has had more than a touch of that. On January 20, 1997, he took the oath of office for the second time. Then he strolled down Pennsylvania Avenue hand in hand with Hillary to begin four more years in the White House. The miracle man from Hope, Arkansas, continues his remarkable success story, heading toward that date in history when he becomes the first American President of the twenty-first century.

Names in the News in Clinton's Time

Madeleine K. Albright (1937–):

Named UN ambassador in 1993, she became the first female U.S. secretary of state when Clinton appointed her to head that department for his second term.

William (Bill) Bradley (1943–):

Missouri-born U.S. senator from New Jersey (1979–1996). Civil rights advocate, often mentioned as candidate for U.S. President. Former basketball star with the New York Knickerbockers (1967–1977).

Robert (Bob) Dole (1923–):

U.S. representative from Kansas (1961–1969); U.S. senator (1969–1996); Senate majority leader (1985–1987; 1995–1996). Running mate for Gerald Ford (1976); lost Republican nomination for President in 1988. Retired from Senate and lost election to Clinton (1996).

Mike Espy (1953–):

First African American and first southerner to become secretary of agriculture, appointed by Clinton. First African American congressman elected from Mississippi (1986) in this century.

Michael Jordan (1963–):

New York-born basketball superstar (Chicago Bulls, 1984). Nicknamed "Air," called perhaps the greatest basketball player ever.

Janet Reno (1938–):

Florida-born first female U.S. attorney general. State attorney for Dade County, Florida, at time of her appointment by Clinton.

Donna Shalala (1941–):

Appointed by Clinton as secretary of health and human services. First woman to head a major midwestern state university, she was chancellor of the University of Wisconsin at Madison.

Important Facts and Events in the Terms

of Presidents Thirty-Seven Through Forty-Two

37. Richard Milhous Nixon (1969–1974)

Republican party, age at inauguration, 56

Born: Yorba Linda, California, January 9, 1913

Died: New York City, April 22, 1994

Education; occupation: Whittier College (1934), Duke University
   Law School (1937); lawyer

Family: Thelma Catherine Patricia Ryan (married 1940);
   children: Tricia, Julie

Important events during Nixon's terms:

   1969: SALT (Strategic Arms Limitation) talks begin with Soviet
         Union; American astronaut walks on the moon.

   1972: Nixon visits Russia and Red China; Watergate break-in;
         Nixon reelected.

   1973: Cease-fire in Vietnam; Vice President Agnew resigns;
         Nixon appoints Ford as vice president.

   1974: Administration officials indicted for Watergate;
         under threat of impeachment, Nixon resigns.

38. Gerald Rudolph Ford (1974–1977)

Republican party, age at inauguration, 61

Born: Omaha, Nebraska, July 14, 1913

Education; occupation: University of Michigan (1935),
   Yale Law School (1941); lawyer

Family: Elizabeth Boomer Warren (married 1948);
   children: Michael, Jack, Steven, Susan

Important events during Ford's term:

   1974: U.S. establishes diplomatic relations with East Germany;
         Ford pardons Nixon.

   1975: Communists gain control of Cambodia and South Vietnam;
         Suez Canal reopens after eight years;
         two attempted assassinations on Ford

   1976: U.S. celebrates bicentennial; *Viking I* lands on Mars.

39. James Earl Carter, Jr. (1977–1981)

Democratic party, age at inauguration, 52
Born: Plains, Georgia, October 1, 1924
Education; occupation: U.S. Naval Academy (1946); farmer
Family: Rosalynn Smith (married 1946);
   children: Jack, James III, Jeff, Amy
Important events during Carter's term:
   1977: Energy Department created; Panama Canal treaties signed.
   1978: Camp David Accords signed.
   1979: U.S. recognizes mainland China;
        Iranians take 50 Americans hostage in Teheran.
   1980: U.S. protests Soviet invasion of Afghanistan,
        U.S. boycotts Olympic Games in Moscow.
   1981: Hostages released on Carter's last day as President.

40. Ronald Wilson Reagan (1981–1989)

Republican party, age at inauguration, 69
Born: Tampico, Illinois, February 6, 1911
Education; occupation: Eureka College (1932); sportscaster, actor
Family: Jane Wyman (married 1940, divorced, 1948);
   Nancy Davis (married 1952);
   children: Maureen, Michael, Patti, Ronald
Important events during Reagan's terms:
   1981: Attempted assassination; Sandra O'Connor becomes
        first woman on Supreme Court.
   1982: Vietnam Memorial dedicated.
   1983: U.S. troops invade Grenada; Sally Ride becomes first
        U.S. woman in space; U.S. Embassy bombed in Lebanon.
   1985: U.S.-Soviet Summit in Geneva
   1986: Space Shuttle *Challenger* explodes; funds diverted from
        Iranian arms deal to Nicaraguan contras.
   1987: Reagan submits one trillion dollar budget to Congress;
        200th anniversary of ratification of U.S. Constitution

41. George Herbert Walker Bush (1989–1993)

Republican party, age at inauguration, 64
Born: Milton, Massachusetts, June 12, 1924
Education; occupation: Yale (1948); businessman
Family: Barbara Pierce (married 1945);
   children: George, John, Neil, Marvin, Dorothy
Important events during Bush's term:
    1989: Summit meeting with Gorbachev;
           U.S. troops sent to Panama.
    1990: Summit meeting with Gorbachev; U.S. troops sent to
           Persian Gulf for operations Desert Shield and Desert Storm.

42. William Jefferson Clinton (1993–2001)

Democratic party; age at inauguration, 46
Born: Hope, Arkansas, August 19, 1946
Education; occupation: Georgetown University (1968),
   Yale Law School (1973); teacher (law)
Family: Hillary Rodham (married 1975); children: Chelsea
Important events during Clinton's first term:
    1993: Branch Davidians conflict, Waco, Texas; Whitewater investigations begin; health care reform package presented.
    1994: Congress passes legislation to implement North American Free Trade Agreement (NAFTA), aimed at aiding trade among Mexico, Canada, and the United States; U.S. troops sent to Somalia; U.S. troops sent to Haiti; Clinton signs anticrime bill; Republicans sweep both houses of Congress.
    1995: Bomb explodes outside federal office building in Oklahoma City, killing 169 people; dispute between President and Congress over the federal budget shuts down the government in November and December; U.S. troops sent to Bosnia.
    1996: Oklahoma City bombing trial moved to Denver, Colorado; Congress passes and Clinton signs antiterrorist bill.

Glossary

Alzheimer's disease A degenerative disease of the central nervous system, characterized by memory loss and mental deterioration.

blind trust Arrangement in which a person in power in order to prevent conflict of interest places financial affairs in the hands of another and gives up the right to know about their handling.

born-again One who has been "born again" has experienced a profound revival of personal faith, such as a born-again Christian.

boycott Refusal to deal with a nation, company or organization, in order to force a change in policy or to express disapproval.

conservative In politics, one who adheres to traditional methods or views, usually marked by moderation or caution.

deferment Official postponement of military service.

dyslexia Disorder that inhibits a person's ability to read.

evangelist One who ardently preaches his or her religion through sermons or special services.

glasnost Russian word meaning a spirit of openness.

gridlock Lack of movement; generally used to indicate traffic jams where crossing streets are so blocked that no movement is possible; used in politics to describe a situation between two sides in which no action or progress can be made.

hardliner One who follows the strict course of action, or political party line, without deviation.

hijacker One who takes over an airplane, or other vehicle, and holds the occupants hostage.

hostage A person held against his or her will, generally for ransom or some particular favor.

impeachment A criminal charge brought against a government official, such as the President.

incumbent A government official already in office.

laryngitis Inflammation of the larynx, which contains the vocal cords in humans and most other mammals.

moderate In politics, one who avoids extremes and generally follows a middle-of-the-road course of action.

New South In the late twentieth century, used to mean a change in the region, characterized by racial integration, urban development, ethnic harmony, and liberal politics.

recession A period of reduced economic activity.

Red Scare Intense fear of the former Soviet Union policies, especially during the post-World War II period.

sanctions In politics, an economic or military measure to force a nation to stop violating international law.

savings and loan banks Financial institutions that take in money from citizens and use it generally to grant home mortgages.

scholarship A grant-in-aid to a student, usually from a university or foundation.

segregationist One who believes in keeping the races separate.

sitting President A President who is currently in office.

sting An elaborate undercover game used by police officials to trap criminals.

subpoena A writ demanding that a person appear in court.

Teflon presidency Said of Ronald Reagan because no blame ever "stuck to him," just as food does not stick to a Teflon-coated pan.

terrorist One who uses threats or violence, usually against innocent people, as a means of bringing about his or her wishes

trickle-down economics Reagan's economic theory in which money in the hands of big business will "trickle down" through the levels of society and benefit all.

Further Reading

Blue, Rose and Naden, Corinne J. *Barbara Bush: First Lady.* Enslow, 1991

Boyd, Aaron. *First Lady: The Story of Hillary Rodham Clinton.* Reynolds, 1994

Cole, Michael D. *Bill Clinton: United States President.* Enslow, 1994

Collins, David. *Gerald R. Ford: Thirty-Eighth President of the United States.* Garrett, 1990

Cozic, Charles P., ed. *Politicians and Ethics.* Greenhaven, 1996

Feinberg, Barbara S. *American Political Scandals Past and Present.* Franklin Watts, 1992

Katz, William L. *Great Society to the Reagan Era, 1964-1993.* Raintree Steck-Vaughn, 1993

Larsen, Rebecca. *Richard Nixon: The Rise and Fall of a President.* Franklin Watts, 1991

_____ ___. *Ronald Reagan.* Franklin Watts, 1994

Lucas, Eileen. *Reagan, Bush, and Clinton.* Rourke, 1996

Majure, Janet. *Elections.* Lucent, 1996

Martin, Gene L. and Boyd, Aaron. *Bill Clinton: President from Arkansas.* Tudor, 1993

Mayo, Edith, ed. *The Smithsonian Book of the First Ladies: Their Lives, Times, and Issues.* Holt, 1996

Morin, Isabel V. *Impeaching the President.* Millbrook, 1996

Morris, Jeffery B. *Reagan Way.* Lerner, 1995

Reische, Diana. *Electing a U.S. President.* Franklin Watts, 1992

Smith, Betsy C. *Jimmy Carter, President.* Walker, 1986

Stefoff, Rebecca. *George H. Bush: Forty-First President of the United States.* Garrett, 1995

_____. *Richard M. Nixon: Thirty-Seventh President of the United States.* Garrett, 1995

Sullivan, George. *George Bush.* Simon and Schuster, 1989

Westerfield, Scott. *Watergate.* Silver Burdett, 1991

Wright, David. *Vietnam War,.* Raintree Steck-Vaughn, 1995

Index

Numbers in **bold** indicate pictures.

A

Achille Lauro, 50
Adams, Abigail, 5–6
Adams, John, 5
Afghanistan, 34
Agnew, Spiro, 12, 16, 17, 20
Albright, Madeleine K., 86
Aldrin, Edwin, **12**
Apollo 11, 13, 19
Aristide, Jean-Bertrand, 81
Arkansas, 74–76
Armstrong, Neil, **12,** 13, 19
Arthur, Chester, 20
assassination attempts
    against Gerald R. Ford, 24
    against Ronald Reagan,
        46–47

B

Baird, Zoe, 79
Begin, Menachem, 34, **35**
Bentsen, Lloyd, 63
Berlin, Irving, 42
Berlin Wall, **67**
Bernstein, Carl, 15
Betty Ford Clinic, 22
Bradley, Bill, 86
Brady, James, 47, 56, **84**
Branch Davidians, 80
Bray, Linda, 66
Brown, Edmund "Pat," 12, 44
Buchanan, Pat, 69, 78
Burger, Warren, 23
Bush, Barbara Pierce, 59, 60,
    60, 64–65, **65,** 69
Bush, Dorothy Walker, 58,
    60
Bush, George Herbert Walker,
    37, 51, **56,** 57–69, **77,** 83
    as ambassador to China,
        61, **61**

as ambassador to United
    Nations, 60
as CIA director, 61–62
and collapse of
    communism, 66–67
defeat of, 69, 78
early career, 60
and election of 1980, 62
election of, to presidency,
    63, 64
evaluation of, 69
fact summary for, 89
family of, 58–60, **60**
in House of
    Representatives, 60
and Nicaragua, 66
and Richard M. Nixon, 60,
    61
"no new taxes" promise
    of, 64, 65
and Panama, 65–66
and Persian Gulf War,
    67–68, **68,** 77
personality of, 57-58
and Ronald Reagan, 46
and savings and loan
    crisis, 65
as vice president, 62–63
as war hero, 57
youth, 58–59
Bush, George W. (son of
    George Bush), 59, **60**
Bush, John (Jeb), 59, **60**
Bush, Marvin, 59, **60**
Bush, Neil, 59, **60,** 65
Bush, Prescott S., 58
Bush, Robin, 59

C

California, 44
Camp David Accords, 34–35,
    35
Carter, Amy, 30, **33**
Carter, Billy, 28

Carter, Gloria, 28
Carter, Jack, 30
Carter, James, III, 30
Carter, James Earl ("Jimmy"),
    Jr., 25, 27–38, 40, 62, 80
    accomplishments of, 33–35
    and Camp David Accords,
        34–35, **35**
    and Carter Doctrine, 36–37
    and Carter Presidential
        Center, 37
    and Congress, 33
    as dark horse candidate,
        31–32
    in debate with Ronald
        Reagan, **45**
    defeat of, 37
    and desegregation, 30–31
    early career, 28–29, **29**
    election of, to presidency,
        33
    evaluation of, 37–38
    fact summary for, 88
    family of, 30
    and Gerald R. Ford, 32
    as governor of Georgia,
        30–31
    and hostage crisis, 35–36,
        50
    inauguration of, 33, **33**
    informality of, 27
    and New South, 31
    and Panama Canal treaty,
        34
    personality and character
        of, 27
    in retirement, 37, **38**
    and Soviet invasion of
        Afghanistan, 34
    in World War II, 28
    youth, 27–28
Carter, James Earl, Sr., 28, 29
Carter, Jeff, 30
Carter, Lillian Goody, 28

Carter, Rosalynn Smith, 29–30, **33,** 37
Carter, Ruth, 28
Carter Doctrine, 36–37
Castro, Fidel, 55
Central Intelligence Agency (CIA), 61–62
Challenger disaster, 52
Chamorro, Violeta, 66
"Checkers" speech, 11
China, 12, 14, 60, 61
Churchill, Winston, 58
CIA. *See* Central Intelligence Agency
Clinton, Chelsea, **78,** 78–79
Clinton, Hillary Rodham, 69, 75, **75,** 77, 78, **78,** 81, 82, 85
Clinton, Roger (half brother of Bill Clinton), 72, 76
Clinton, Roger (stepfather of Bill Clinton), 72
Clinton, Virginia Cassidy Blythe, 71–72
Clinton, William Jefferson ("Bill"), 4–6, 56, 68, 71–85
  accomplishments of, 84–85
  allergies of, 79
  appearance of, 79
  and Brady Bill, **84**
  as demonstrator against Vietnam War, 74, 77
  and education reform, 76
  election of, to presidency, 69, 78
  fact summary for, 89
  foreign policy initiatives of, 80, 81
  and gays in military, 79–80
  government shutdowns under, 81–82
  as governor of Arkansas, 75–77, **75**
  health care reform plan of, 81

inauguration of, 4, 5, **5**
and Nannygate, 79
as presidential candidate, 77, **77**
reelection of, 83
support for, 83–84
as university student, 73–74
and Waco raid, 80
and Whitewater affair, 80–81, 82
youth, 71–73, **73**
"coattails," 76
Cold War, 9
Coleman, Julia, 28
Collins, Judy, 79
Collins, Michael, **12**
Colson, Charles, 16
Committee to Reelect the President (CREEP), 15
communism, collapse of, 66–67
Connally, John, 23
Coolidge, Calvin, 20
CREEP. *See* Committee to Reelect the President
Cuomo, Mario, 70, **70**

D

Danforth, John, 69
Davis, Patti, 43
Dean, John, 15, 16
Dewey, Thomas, 22
Diem, Ngo Dinh, 13
Dole, Elizabeth H., 70
Dole, Robert ("Bob"), 25, 32, 70, 82, 83, 86
Douglas, Helen Gahagan, 10
Dukakis, Michael S., 63, 64
dyslexia, 65

E

Eagleton, Thomas, 14
East Germany, 66
Ehrlichman, John D., 16

Eisenhower, David, **9**
Eisenhower, Dwight D., 10–12, 34, 54
Eisenhower, Mamie, **9**
election
  of 1952, 10–11
  of 1964, 44
  of 1968, 12
  of 1972, 14
  of 1976, 25, 45
  of 1980, 25, 37, 45–46, 62
  of 1984, 51
  of 1988, 63, 64
  of 1992, 69, 78
  of 1996, 83
El Salvador, 50
"enemies list," 15
Ervin, Sam, 15
Espy, Mike, 86
Ethiopia, 37

F

Ferraro, Geraldine, 51, 56, **56**
Fillmore, Millard, 20
Flowers, Gennifer, 77
Ford, Elizabeth "Betty," 18, 22, **22**
Ford, Gayle, **22**
Ford, Gerald Rudolf (stepfather of Gerald Ford), 20, 21
Ford, Gerald Rudolph, 17, 18, 20–25, 45, 58, 61, 62, 86
  assassination attempts against, 24
  debate gaffe of, 32
  defeat of, 23, 25
  evaluation of, 25
  fact summary for, 87
  family of, 22, **22**
  in House of Representatives, 22–23
  pardon of Richard Nixon by, 23
  in retirement, 25

supposed clumsiness of, 24
swearing in of, as
    President, 23
as unelected President, 20
as vice president, 23
and Vietnam Conflict,
    23–24
in World War II, 21
youth, 20–21, **21**
Ford, John, 22, **22**
Ford, Michael, 22, **22**
Ford, Steven, 22, **22**
Ford, Susan, 22, **22**
Foster, Jodie, 47
Foster, Vincent, 80
Fromme, Lynette "Squeaky,"
    24
Fulbright, William J., 73, 74

G

gays in military, 79–80
Germany, 66, **66**
glasnost, 50
Goals 2000, 85
Goldwater, Barry, 44
Gorbachev, Mikhail, 49–50,
    54, 67
Gore, Al, 77
Grenada, invasion of, 49, **49**
Grossman, Robert, **56**

H

Habitat for Humanity, 37, **38**
Haig, Alexander M., Jr., 56
Haiti, 37, 81
Haldeman, H. R., 16, **16**
Harris, Patricia R., 39
Head Start, 84–85
health care reform, 81
Hinckley, John W., 47
Hiss, Alger, 10
Holden, William, 43, **43,** 56
Hoover, Herbert, 40, 64
House Un-American
    Activities Committee, 9

Hufstedler, Shirley M., 39
Humphrey, Hubert H., 12, 39
Hussein, Saddam, 67

I

impeachment, 17
Inauguration Day, 4
Intermediate Range Nuclear
    Forces (INF) Treaty, 50
Iran, 54
Iran-Contra scandal, 52–53,
    62–63
Iran hostage crisis, 35–36, **36,**
    45, 46, 50
Iraq, 54, 67–68. *See also*
    Persian Gulf War

J

Jackson, Henry, 31
Japan, 85
Johnson, Andrew, 20, 40
Johnson, Lyndon B., 16–17,
    20, 23, 44
Jordan, Michael, 86

K

Kennedy, John F., 12, 16, 23,
    73, **73**
Kennedy, Ted, 55
Kent State University, 13
Khomeini, Ayatollah, 35, 46
Khrushchev, Nikita, **11,** 11–12
King, Coretta Scott, 32
King, Leslie Lynch, Sr., 20–21
King, Martin Luther, Jr., 74
Kirkpatrick, Jeane J., 62
Kissinger, Henry, 25, **26**
Korean airline disaster, 49
Kuwait, 54

L

Lebanon, 50, 52
Libya, 51
Liddy, G. Gordon, 16
Lincoln, Abraham, 58

Lin Peng, **61**
Luce, Clare Booth, 19
Lurie, Ranan, **26**

M

Marshall, Brenda, **43**
Mayaguez incident, 23–24
McAuliffe, Christa, 52, **52**
McCarthy, Joseph R., 9
McDougal, James, 80
McGovern, George, 14, 19
Meir, Golda, **26**
Miskito Indians, 37
Mitchell, John, 19
Mondale, Walter F., 32, 37, 39,
    51
Monroe, Marilyn, 58
moon landing, **12,** 12–13
Moore, Sara Jane, 24

N

NAFTA. *See* North American
    Free Trade Agreement
Nannygate, 79
NATO. *See* North Atlantic
    Treaty Organization
new Republicans, 53
New South, 31
Nicaragua, 50, 52, 66
Nixon, Francis, 7
Nixon, Hannah Milhous, 7–8
Nixon, Julie, **9**
Nixon, Richard Milhous,
    7–18, 20, 25, 45
accomplishments of, 12–13
as anticommunist, 9–10
and George Bush, 60, 61
"Checkers" speech of, 11
complexity of, 7
early career, 8–9
and election of 1952, 10–11
and election of 1960, 12
election of, to presidency,
    12
fact summary for, 87

family of, **9**
as gubernatorial
    candidate, 12
in House of
    Representatives, 9–10,
    10
impeachment proceedings
    against, 17
and moon landing, **12,**
    12–13
and Nixon Doctrine, 12
pardon of, 23, 32
reelection of, 14
resignation of, **17,** 17–18
in retirement, 18
as vice president, 11–12
and Vietnam Conflict,
    13–14
and Watergate scandal,
    14–17
in World War II, 9
youth, 7–8, **8**
Nixon, Thelma "Pat" Ryan, 8,
    9, 17, 18
Nixon, Tricia, **9**
Nixon Doctrine, 12
Noriega, Manuel Antonio,
    65–66
North American Free Trade
    Agreement (NAFTA),
    85
North Atlantic Treaty
    Organization (NATO), 9

O

oath of office, 4
O'Connor, Sandra Day, 56
Olympic Games (1980), 34
Operation Desert Storm, 67

P

Panama, 65–66
Panama Canal treaty, 34
Pan Am flight 103, **50,** 50–51
Perot, Ross, 68, **68, 77,** 78

Persian Gulf
    and Carter Doctrine, 36–37
    Ronald Reagan and, 54
Persian Gulf War, 67–68, **68,**
    77
Pierce, Franklin, 58
Pierce, Marvin, 59
Poland, 66
Powell, Colin, 37, 70, 80

Q

Qaddafi, Muammar al-, 51, 55
Quayle, Dan, 63–64
Quayle, Marilyn, 69, 78

R

Reagan, John (brother of
    Ronald Reagan), 41
Reagan, John (father of
    Ronald Reagan), 41
Reagan, Maureen, 42
Reagan, Michael, 42
Reagan, Nancy Davis, 43, **43,**
    46, 55
Reagan, Nelle Wilson, 41
Reagan, Ronald, Jr., 43
Reagan, Ronald Wilson,
    40–55, 62, 64, 76
    acting background of,
        40–44
    age of, 46, 51
    assassination attempt
        against, 46–47
    budget deficit under, 48
    George Bush and, 57
    and *Challenger* disaster, 52
    conservatism of, 42–44
    in debate with Jimmy
        Carter, **45**
    divorce of, 42
    early career, 41–44, **42**
    and election of 1964, 44
    and election of 1976, 25, 45
    election of, to presidency,
        37, 45–46

evaluation of, 55
fact summary for, 88
and Mikhail Gorbachev, **54**
as governor of California,
    44–45
as "Great Communicator,"
    42
and Grenada invasion, 49,
    49
and Iran-Contra scandal,
    52–53
military buildup under, 48
and new Republicans, 53
and Richard Nixon, 23
and Reaganomics, 47–48
and Red Scare, 43
reelection of, 51–52
and release of hostages, 46
in retirement, 54–55
second marriage of, 43, **43**
and Soviet Union, 45,
    49–50
"Teflon Presidency" of, 53
and terrorism, 50–51
youth, 41
Reaganomics, 47–48
Red Scare, 9–10, 43
Regan, Donald, 46
Reno, Janet, 79, 80, 86
Rhodes, Cecil John, 74
Richards, Ann, 64
Rockefeller, John D., 26
Rockefeller, Nelson A., 23, 26,
    61
Roosevelt, Eleanor, 30
Roosevelt, Franklin D., 4, 53,
    83
Roosevelt, Theodore, 20, 58

S

Sadat, Anwar, 25, **26,** 34–35,
    35
Sanders, Carl, 30
Schwarzkopf, H. Norman, 67
Screen Actors Guild, 43

SDI. *See* Strategic Defense Initiative
Shalala, Donna, 86
Socks, 79
Sorel, Edward, **19**
Soviet Union, 9, 14
and Carter Doctrine, 36–37
collapse of, 67
invasion of Afghanistan by, 34
Ronald Reagan and, 45, 49–50
Stark (U.S. frigate), 54
Strategic Defense Initiative (SDI), 48
Straus, Robert, 69
student unrest, 13
supply-side economics, 47–48
Supreme Court, 30, 56

T

Taft, William Howard, 64
Taiwan, 60
terrorism, 50–51
Thatcher, Margaret, 55
Thomas, Mrs. Willis Manning, **29**

Three Mile Island accident, 33
Three Servicemen (sculpture), 14
trickle-down economics, 47–48
Truman, Harry, 20, 40
Twenty-Fifth Amendment, 16, 20, 23, 62
Tyler, John, 20

U

Udall, Morris, 31
United Nations, 60, 67

V

Van Buren, Martin, 64
Vietnam Conflict, **24**
William J. Clinton and, 74, 77
Gerald R. Ford and, 23
Richard M. Nixon and, 13–14
pardon of draft evaders in, 33
Vietnam Veterans Memorial, 14
Vietnam Women's Memorial, 14

W

Waco raid, 80
Walesa, Lech, 66
Walker, George Herbert, 58
Wallace, George, 19, **19**, 30, 32
Warren Commission, 22–23
Washington, George, 4–6, 8
Watergate scandal, 14–17, **16,** 23, 25
Welty, Eudora, 26
White, Frank, 75–76
White, John, 75
White House, East Room of, 6
Whitewater affair, 80–82
Wood, Kimba, 79
Woodward, Bob, 15
World War II
George Bush in, 57, 59
James Earl Carter in, 28
Gerald R. Ford in, 21
Richard M. Nixon in, 9
Wyman, Jane, 42

Y

Yeltsin, Boris, 67